SRI GARY OLSEN
1948 –

MEETING WITH THE MASTER

SOUL'S
DIVINE JOURNEY

MASTERPATH
THE LIGHT AND SOUND TEACHINGS

SRI GARY OLSEN

Reprinted 2012

ISBN 978-1-885949-07-3

MASTERPATH®
P.O. Box 9035
Temecula, CA 92589-9035
www.masterpath.org

TABLE OF CONTENTS

PREFACE

Soul's divine journey cannot be adequately described, fully encompassed, or completely understood by and through the ordinary intellectual senses of a human being. Many sincere individuals have attempted to do so, but their spiritual pens could only record the depth of their own personal excursions into the mysteries of the created universe. In order to accurately depict and comprehensively portray the numerous stages of soul's divine journey, from its original starting point to its prodigal return, one would be required to personally undertake and traverse this journey of soul to its glorious conclusion. As such, only those who actually complete this ineffable journey, having received firsthand experience, are able to correctly interpret and lay bare in bold print the totality of truth and the rapturous glories of such an epic sojourn.

All Light and Sound Masters have embarked upon this dazzling spiritual journey and have completed its course. Their divine message is universal, inspiring, and uplifting, sweetly pointing to the great truth of soul's eventual liberation and its own inherent divinity. The Masters of Light and Sound have always championed the goals of Self, Spirit, and God Realization, lovingly reminding us that even though we were born as the sons and daughters of humankind, we shall in time transform ourselves into the sons and daughters of God.

The Masters elucidate clearly the cosmological panorama of God's created universe, offering all seekers a precise spiritual road map by which to proceed back to their original starting point. The true Masters diligently accompany their students along the way, deftly guiding, instructing, and protecting each traveling soul in its divine journey homeward. The Masters reveal the great divide between the currents of light and those of Sound, and they unanimously declare that only through initiation into the celestial Sound Current can the soul speedily ascend the ladder of consciousness, effortlessly regaining the heavenly states of consciousness once again.

Within these pages I humbly submit my findings, which are in complete unison with those spiritual Luminaries who have sung before me. In doing so, I openly invite anyone who can resonate and hear the music of my words to raptly listen and to quietly ponder over the melody of truth's song.

Sri Gary Olsen
September 2010

INTRODUCTION

Numerous individuals have concluded that they have already found the absolute truth, and there are even countless more who have little interest in any truth at all. But there remain a rare breed, a select cadre who, even though having held steadfastly to the vision and promise of truth, have not yet seen its present-day manifestation or uncovered the hidden secret of its mystery. Those within this unique group of spiritual truth seekers now have an opportunity, if they are so drawn, to peruse this spiritual introduction to MasterPath, the Divine Teachings of Light and Sound, to clearly see for themselves whether this hidden and elusive truth might be revealed within its pages.

Every deep-thinking seeker desires to solve the riddle of the universe, the dilemma of human existence, and the divine purpose which all must eventually discover and then pursue. In an honest attempt to understand this divine mystery, many have placed an image upon their mental screen and have deeply contemplated the many angles of vision which naturally arise, hoping to finally decipher life's divine meaning. But with every developing insight, an accompanying mental paradox is given birth, and this constant vacillation of the mind deftly neutralizes the seeker's desire to move inward and upward toward one's Source. The mind desperately searches for a shortcut to the final solution, but none is forthcoming, for the mind is saddled with its inherent dualistic tendencies, which fill it with utter helplessness and perplexity. As long as seekers continue to rely only upon the counsel of their own minds, this enigmatic dilemma will continue, for it is not within the mental capacity of the reasoning intellect to discern or interpret aright either the way back to soul's place of origin or the incandescent nature of the absolute truth.

However, this does not mean that absolute truth does not exist, nor that it has never been available or painstakingly articulated to the races inhabiting the globe. Illuminated Saints and Masters from all cultures have, in the past and present times, unfailingly offered this ultimate truth, especially to those few who have had the eyes and ears to clearly perceive and comprehend.

Nevertheless, the pursuit of truth has become externalized, and thus the original Source of truth, which innately resides in the individual, has been minimized or wholly lost. No longer is the individual seen as the repository of truth, for truth has been relegated strictly to the collective whole or a specific institution, whether religious, philosophical, or metaphysical. This is a curious phenomenon, for all Saints have emphasized unanimously that the ultimate truth and its discovery lie within the many folds of the individual's inner consciousness, and without searching within oneself, the luminous nature of truth can never be found.

Therefore, the Saints come not to establish or form a new outer religion, but to introduce and enliven within us the true inner religion. The soul has externalized itself and has endlessly worshiped buildings, shrines, and temples; it has read and studied various scriptures from around the world; it has relied on fasts, rites, and ceremonies; it has worshiped idols made of stone; and it has paid homage to past prophets, incarnations, and men of God. But the soul has failed to apply and direct its worship and devotion to the proper quarters of Spirit's abode. In truth, our devotion and adoration need only be applied to the indwelling Spiritual Current, for this is true religion. The soul is part and parcel of this melodious Spiritual Current, and the Spiritual Current is the manifested Essence of the Creator. All three exist within the chambers of the human body, and consequently, our reverential method of devotion should be solely directed to this indwelling Trinity of soul, Spirit, and God, which are reposed within the inner temple just above and behind the two eyes.

A Light and Sound Path specializes in clarifying this inner spiritual journey and ultimate search for the self and God within one, and indisputably maintains that true liberation and salvation can only be understood and attained by reversing the search from an outward pursuit to one of inward enlightenment. If you wish to retrace your steps in order to ultimately realize your innate spiritual origin, I lovingly encourage you to investigate the MasterPath, the Divine Teachings of Light and Sound, for only your own firsthand experience of soul's divine journey can put an end to all uncertainty and speculation concerning the Godhead, simultaneously revealing the secret purpose and hidden meaning of your human existence.

CHAPTER ONE

THE ORIGIN OF THE
ETERNAL LIGHT AND SOUND

More than ever before, truth seekers around the globe are in search of a pure and fail-safe Path, one that not only can be personally verified and tested for its authenticity, but which also transcends the traditional religious and metaphysical beliefs that have been imposed and foisted upon the minds of men and women everywhere. Clearly, a growing spiritual hunger has seized the minds of truth seekers, but the age-old questions of "what is truth" and "where is it to be found" still gnaw and linger within the chambers of their innermost being. Who can be trusted, and furthermore, what spiritual doctrine, if any, can lay bare the esoteric truths and flawlessly guide the indwelling soul back to its Homeland? These seem to be the pressing needs and insurmountable challenges of all spiritual enthusiasts who are presently inhabiting this planet.

In order for the soul to first discover and then commence its divine journey back to its Source, the correct spiritual method, a competent and fully realized Guru, and the purest form of the spiritual Essence of God are needed. Thus, the Divine Teachings of Light and Sound have been eternally present to fulfill these three paramount requirements of a true Teaching, a true Master, and the true spiritual Sound Current.

The Light and Sound Teachings are not a religion, philosophy, occult teaching, or a metaphysical doctrine.

1

Neither are they an extension of any major religion in existence today, for the Teachings of the Light and Sound are unique unto themselves. They existed long before the march of time and remain pristinely unpolluted by the hand of humanity. The Light and Sound Teachings have been referred to by many names, such as the Teachings of the Saints, the Divine Science of Light and Sound, soul's divine journey, and Surat Shabda Yoga, or the yoga of the Sound Current in the Eastern tradition.

When the doctrine of Light and Sound is referred to as the Teachings of the Saints, reference is being made to the universal message of all past and present Masters, each of whom has exclusively given the same identical Teaching to humanity. All true Masters have embraced the one Teaching, the one truth, for each has unquestionably followed this very Light and Sound method back into their own Self and God-realized states.

When the Light and Sound Teachings are being defined as a Divine Science, it is meant to convey the ability of the individual to know truth through personal experience, the ability to scientifically prove and repeat any spiritual experience to yourself, much like physical scientists do in their laboratories. With verifiable results spontaneously flowing into your own inner consciousness, faith and belief, along with hope and speculation, become somewhat meaningless, for you are now afforded the opportunity to personally experience these higher levels of consciousness rather than viewing them from afar.

When the Light and Sound Teachings are characterized as soul's divine journey, it is meant to convey the sequential steps that must be taken to transcend the binding conditions placed upon the soul inhabiting the lower worlds. These conditions include all laws of duality, such as the karmic principle working through the conscious, subconscious, and unconscious minds. Each of these aspects of the overall mind will ultimately be penetrated and completely transcended on the journey of soul.

And when the Light and Sound Teachings are being defined as the yoga of the Sound Current, reference is being made to the spiritual practice of bringing the soul of the disciple into union with the melodious spiritual Current of Sound. In the Eastern tradition, many yogic practices have come and gone, but three main branches exist today. the yoga of action, the yoga of bhakti, and the yoga of knowledge. All yogic paths fall into these general divisions, such as Laya, Bhakti, Hatha, Raja, Kundalini, and Karma yoga. Yogic practices that emphasize bodily postures alone do not qualify, for true yoga, in strict spiritual parlance, refers to spiritual practice. The highest and most sublime yoga known is Surat Shabda Yoga, which translated means the spiritual practice (yoga) of merging the soul (surat) into the Sound Current (Shabda). So, in the terminology of the East, MasterPath is Surat Shabda Yoga, and no higher yoga exists.

When the soul comes into the orbit of the spiritual essence called Sound, this divine Current becomes audible to the ear of soul. Light is knowledge, but Sound is the original spiritual Essence of which knowledge is a mere part. Light alone will illuminate the mind, but only Sound can deliver the soul back to its original Homeland. Both knowledge and Spirit are needed to bring soul into its own Self and God Realization, but light comes first, and it is then followed by Sound. Sound is the exclusive heritage of the Saints, while light alone is predominantly the heritage of religious orders, pseudo gurus, yogic instruction, and psychic and metaphysical endeavor. Light, or knowledge, will enlighten the mind, but cannot deliver the soul into the portals of the heavenly consciousness, for light is simply a derivative of the mind, while Sound issues forth exclusively from the soul. The Saints of all times have emphasized that both the light and Sound are necessary to secure the highest realization, and thus, the Light and Sound Teachings are classified as the Teachings of the Saints.

The core philosophy of the Divine Teachings of Light and Sound centers around these twin pillars of knowledge and realization. Light is knowledge, which sustains the mind, while Sound is the spiritual Current that sustains the soul. Through the knowledge of the light, the way back Home can be read about in the scriptures or talked about from the pulpits, but the actual journey homeward cannot be taken. Knowledge sheds light, but it fails in literally taking the soul upon and through the divine journey. In contrast, the Sound is the father of all light and is not confined to just knowledge or academic speculation, for the Sound is the supreme Essence emanating from the Divine Deity Itself. Upon this Current did all life devolve, and upon this same Current will all life evolve. The Sound Current is the controlling life force of the entire creation, molding and framing all existence from the highest to the lowest reaches of God's universal body. The Sound Current has been referenced in nearly every existing religion and divine scripture known to humankind, and has been termed the Word, Sound, Kalma, Naad, Nam, Shabda, Sraosha, Logos, and Udgit.

A light path can be traveled alone, while a Sound Path requires a guide or teacher. A light path, if diligently followed to the end, will bestow illumination and enlightenment to the mind, while in contrast, a Sound Path will crown the traveling soul with Self and God Realization. A light path will take one to the origin of the mind located in the realm of the universal mind power. But a Sound Path will transport the soul above and beyond the realm of mind into the glorified atmosphere of the heavenly Kingdom, known as Sat Lok, or the true Home of soul. A light path cannot eradicate the karmic obligations straddling the infant soul, while a Sound Path effortlessly and expediently obliterates all existing karmic debt.

When reference is being made to a light path, it is to be understood that this includes any teaching which exclusively adorns the mind and its associated energies. The very origin of light itself resides in the second level of Heaven, or Trikuti, as this realm is the repository of all divine knowledge. It is here that the mind finds its highest expression, and thus, at this level it is oftentimes referred to as the divine mind, or the universal mind, which corresponds with the attainment of cosmic consciousness. These above descriptions all revolve within the mental orbit of light, or knowledge, which is a product of the universal mind power. The salient point here is that the origin of true spirituality is a region which exists far above the realm of light alone. While the light can nourish the mind, only Sound can nourish the soul. Therefore, if the spiritual principle of Sound is not predominately expounded upon by a particular path, then that path, no matter what it may be, is a light path in some degree. In such a scenario, the mind will supplant the soul, the light will outcreate the Sound, the universal mind power will usurp the throne, and the presiding deity of the mental realms will be extolled as the highest lord of all.

In contrast, the Light and Sound Masters, coupled with the Divine Teachings, offer the true seeker a far broader perspective, which will continue to increase in scope and sequence until soul can once again reclaim its divine origin. All forms of external religion, all of the various levels of philosophical thought, the differing degrees of yoga, New Age beliefs, and all psychic practices such as healings, aura adjusting, past-life regression, spiritualism, trance channeling, and mediumship, along with astral and mental projection, are considered light paths to the Masters of Light and Sound doctrine. In all of these examples, the mind, in one of its three phases, is being worshiped and mistaken for the soul, which means that only the universal mind power and its psychic power flows have been aroused and activated.

None of these above-mentioned methods reach beyond the realm of Trikuti, and most originate within the astral region, the first inner realm just above this physical plane. All of this is well and fine, that is, if you only wish to evolve the higher mind. The true Spirit, however, remains untouched in a mental scenario such as this, for all psychic practice, prayer, meditation, and worship can only invoke the higher powers of the divine mind and its associated currents. This becomes the glaring discrepancy found within all light paths, and it can be simply defined as an individual's inability to access the soul and true Spirit, or Sound, within one's own inner consciousness.

Thus, the doctrine of Light and Sound is unparalleled and peerless in what it offers the spiritual aspirant. This Teaching clearly differentiates between the soul and mind, offers a precise road map through the multifaceted levels and planes of the inner worlds, and furnishes the student with a Master Soul who instructs, guides, and fully escorts the infant soul from the confines of the human consciousness into the august goals of Self and God Realization. The Light and Sound doctrine is unquestionably the most descriptive, comprehensive, and all-inclusive spiritual Teaching known to humankind.

Every true Saint and Master who has ever visited this globe has preached and sung the glories of this incomparable and ineffable Teaching. While every known religion and spiritual path has had a beginning, and thus an end, the Light and Sound doctrine has existed since before the dawn of time. This divine method of returning soul back to its original starting point is not man-made, but God-made, and was instilled in the heart of soul long before its advent into this physical world. The Lord of the soul, or the Absolute Creator of all, has not left the soul's return journey back to Its bosom in the hands of a well-intended human being, but has etched the divine journey into the very essence of soul. God is one, truth is one, and soul is one. So too is the Way which unerringly leads back to soul's Homeland.

In our spiritual marketplace within the world at large, over a thousand different names exist for both identifying and defining God, but the Supreme Deity still remains one. Likewise, there are thousands of separate paths, consisting of religions, philosophies, metaphysical endeavors, and the psychic arts. In such a labyrinth of multiplicity, the shining Path to the ultimate Kingdom still remains one. It is only the universal mind power, along with its corresponding individual mind in humankind, that has taken the one name of God and turned it into many, and similarly, the one Path has been divided into many.

Nevertheless, the Masters of these Light and Sound Teachings have no enmity or ill feelings toward anyone or any path, as they view all teachings, no matter what they may entail, as part and parcel of the overall school of spirituality. Each and every teaching has its part to play, for souls exist at every level known, whether high or low. Thus, through necessity, all must have some form of guidance and instruction that is applicable to their own relative level of consciousness.

In the fullness of time, all souls, regardless of their current state of consciousness or level of unfoldment, will attain the highest realizations and re-enter the heavenly Kingdom. Complete annihilation of the soul or being cast into an irreversible and eternal damnation are religious theories that have no reality in the Teachings of the Saints.

All souls are drops from the same eternal Ocean of Bliss and Love and, as such, have irrefutably been dyed in the hue of the Almighty Creator. Each soul will in time enter its own Self and God Realization and gloriously emerge as a perfected being. In light of this great truth and spiritual promise, all people, places, and things exist within a perfect set of circumstances, and no judgment or prejudice can be applied to them. The spark of spiritual essence that lights up every human being who has ever come into this world will one day experience the wonders of complete spiritual illumination. Every soul originally departed from the lofty levels of the Lord's spiritual Kingdom, and back to this heavenly Kingdom shall all souls eventually return.

Therefore, when considering a spiritual exodus such as this, one in which the soul consciously traverses through the regions of matter, emotion, and mental thought, it is not difficult to understand that it involves an incomprehensible length of time. A spiritual metamorphosis of this magnitude certainly requires more than the span of one lifetime, and this gives rise to the inexorable laws of karma and reincarnation, which are precise and exact. It is not someone else's sin that binds us, but only our own acts and causes, and thus the law of karma is perfectly just in its application. The karmic law basically states that all good and bad karmas are the result of our own past actions, and so these actions can be rectified at any time we choose. This is strictly an individual matter, and not one that concerns the collective whole of humanity.

The karmic actions of an individual, whether good or not so good, accrue over the course of an individual's lifetimes, and in subsequent incarnations, these prior karmic obligations influence the individual's present-day experience. In this way, perfect justice is metered out, for no other power or entity can dictate what an individual's past, present, or future conditions in various lifetimes may be. Only our own individual choices come into play. Therefore, the religious concept of original sin that has been fed to the teeming masses, as well as the belief that there is only one life to live, find no reality in the doctrine of Light and Sound.

As stated previously, the Teachings of Light and Sound are presented as a spiritual science because all truth must be conclusive and verifiable. If truth cannot be proven to oneself through firsthand experience, then mere speculation, vague hope, and blind faith must be employed. Nothing is to be accepted until you have seen or experienced it for yourself. It is not someone else's truth or viewpoint that needs to be accepted, but only your own hard-won conclusions. See for yourself, and then doubt and uncertainty can have no place within your mental atmosphere, and the way to truth's door will be made clear and luminous to you. Science is accepted in our present world only because the subject matter can be repeatedly proven, and so too should each seeker approach the subject of true spirituality in like manner. In this way, all deceit, all misinformation, and all half-baked ideas and opinions are put to the touchstone of scientific experimentation, clearly revealing what is absolute truth or mere illusion.

The Light and Sound Teachings can be followed by all people, whether old or young, male or female, and regardless of race, academic background, or creed. The Path leading back to soul's original Homeland is simply open to one and all, for it is divinely innate in all living beings. And as well, the Divine Creator has always ensured that there is at least one Living Master, and sometimes several, at any given time upon our planet, for there is no question that if the need for a Master was present in the past, this same need most certainly exists in contemporary times.

At the heart of these Light and Sound Teachings is the clarion call for each soul to realize one's own indelible connection to God the Oversoul, and to ultimately reclaim one's true spiritual inheritance as soul. We are all sons and daughters of God, and thus, each of you is an eventual Master in your own right.

CHAPTER TWO

SOUL'S DIVINE OBJECTIVE

There is neither a beginning nor an end, and there has never been a time when the soul did not exist. Soul is immortal, eternally divine, and imperishable. It is all-knowing, infinite in wisdom and love, and is a by-product of the unfathomable Creator of all. Soul is without blemish or sin; it is formless, genderless, and a fully bona fide child of God. To ultimately realize the soul, the true self within you, is termed Self Realization, and the realization of this true self's indelible connection to God the Oversoul is termed God Realization, the ultimate purpose and attainment of life.

In truth, we are not the human body, we cannot be defined through emotional characteristics or behavior, nor can we be truly identified by the mind and its multiplicity of ideas, thoughts, and opinions. Our true identity is soul, which has nothing whatsoever to do with race, name, creed, or nationality. The true spiritual self is completely unique when compared to these secondary identifications and is absolutely separate from them. Thus, to ferret out this divine being from all else is the entire purpose and ultimate objective of spiritual evolution. Self and God Realization are categorically different in every regard from the popular spiritual attainments known to the world at large. Such levels as being saved in the church, illumination, enlightenment, or cosmic consciousness are all lesser degrees of spiritual attainment when compared to Self and God

Realization, for they deal exclusively with the mind rather than the individual soul.

The divine soul that innately resides within each individual cannot extricate or identify itself under the normal conditions of life, for it is enveloped within mind and matter, and the lofty goal of Self Realization is literally impossible to achieve under such circumstances. The mental diseases of greed, anger, lust, attachment, and vanity serve as barriers to the soul's desire to realize itself because they overwhelmingly engage the physical senses with material objects and desires. With the five physical senses engaged as such, the mental senses become attached to the pleasure that is derived from them, and this basically means that the mind is looking downward and has substituted the pleasure principle for true spiritual bliss and realization. Thus, the mind in turn entraps the spiritual senses, and our spiritual identity is lost. Therefore, according to the Saints and Masters alike, Self Realization is the first major goal to be attained on the soul's divine journey back to its Homeland.

However, the method by which the soul comes to realize itself as distinctly different from the body, emotions, and mind is far easier to describe than achieve. While in the body and the human consciousness, the soul can be identified and recognized as the quality of attention. To free this attention from the influences of mind and matter is the first spiritual objective, but the difficulty lies in the fact that this attention has been submerged and totally controlled by the conscious and subconscious minds for numerous incarnations. Likewise, the attention has been overpowered and entrapped by endless karmic conditions, for all of an individual's tendencies and proclivities are based on past karma, including those developed in one's present lifetime. Mind and matter are wholly comprised of karma and are antithetical to all things spiritual. Therefore, it is absolutely mandatory that the spiritual student transcend the material and mental worlds if one wishes to experience the lofty levels of Self and God Realization.

The entire creation, which is often referred to as God's universal body, can be divided into nine distinct levels of differentiated consciousness, with each ascending level becoming purer and more refulgent than the one below. Above the physical plane, these spiritual regions are known as levels of Heaven, and there are eight realms of heavenly consciousness in all. This entire cosmological structure consisting of these nine distinct levels of consciousness is called the macrocosm, and it is comprised in ascending order as follows: physical plane, astral plane, Trikuti (causal/mental plane), Daswan Dwar, Bhanwar Gupha, Sat Lok, Alakh Lok, Agam Lok, and Anami Lok.

The heavenly paradise to the majority of the religions is situated in the astral sphere, which is known as the first level of Heaven. Enlightened souls such as yogis, yogishwars, and those who have attained cosmic consciousness can achieve the second level of Heaven in Trikuti. The third level of Heaven, or Daswan Dwar, hosts only the Self-realized beings, while those who attain Spiritual Realization gain entry into Bhanwar Gupha, the fourth level of Heaven. God Realization, or the attainment of true Sainthood, occurs in the fifth level of Heaven called Sat Lok, which is the true spiritual Home of soul. The remaining three regions just above this astute realm encompass all that eternity embraces and possesses, and they are reserved solely for perfected souls. The level of Sat Lok, or the fifth level of Heaven, was soul's original starting place, and soul then devolved into the worlds of mind and matter upon the Divine's descending creative wave. Evolution involves the soul riding this same creative wave, but now in its ascending and evolutionary cycle back to Sat Lok, the original abode of soul.

Each human being is actually a microcosm of this great macrocosm, meaning that each individual is an exact duplicate of the macrocosm, but in miniature form. All nine regions within God's universal body are perfectly reflected within the framework of the human body. Each human being is a carbon copy of the great outlying universe of God, and as such, has nine spiritual regions within one's own individual cosmology. This means that we can communicate with any part of the outlying universe by simply retreating to our own inner universe, and in this way, the Supreme Deity maintains a perfect means of communication with Its entire creation. All things exist within the microcosm of the individual, including all levels of Heaven, all karmic accounts, all three minds, and the higher Trinity of soul, Spirit, and God.

The first three planes in the lower worlds, the physical, astral, and causal/mental planes, are dominated and ruled by the mind of humankind. So the soul, or attention, must first free itself from the mundane conscious mind on this physical plane; it must then free the attention from the subconscious mind in the astral worlds, and ultimately free the attention from the unconscious mind in the causal/mental plane. When these three minds are purified and transcended, the soul automatically enters Self Realization and truly recognizes itself and its own unique divinity for the first time.

The initial requirement is to retrieve the scattered attention from the human consciousness and direct it to the focus behind the two eyes, which has been termed by past Saints as the single eye, the third eye, or the tisra til. This single eye resides in the astral plane, or the first level of Heaven. However, this spiritual method of collecting the scattered and diffused attention currents from the body and focusing them at the third eye must be overseen and orchestrated by a divinely appointed Master, or Sat Guru (true Teacher). To attempt this feat on your own is not recommended, for too many unseen forces and powers within your own conscious and subconscious minds do not want the soul to succeed. It must be emphasized that only a true Master of Light and Sound can teach the method of merging the soul into the Sound Current, for no minister, priest, or pseudo guru of light is qualified to do so. In fact, this cherished attainment of the third eye within our own constitution is not even known to most conventional religions or metaphysical paths, let alone practiced.

There are six major stations within the physical body, which are called chakras, and humanity as a whole is situated at the second chakra, or the reproductive center. Most paths known to humankind do not ascend any higher than the fourth chakra at the heart; fewer still reach the fifth chakra at the throat, and very few teach about the ascending levels beyond the first five chakras in the body, except for a Path with a legitimate and competent Master at the helm. Therefore, the chela, or student of the Master, strives diligently to follow the true Master's guidance and counsel, with the aim of rending the veil over one's own third eye aperture. When the soul has escaped the physical consciousness and enters the astral plane within one's own constitution, an extraordinary event transpires. The soul of the disciple rendezvous with the Inner Master just above a region in the astral realm termed the stars, sun, and moon worlds. From this point onward, the soul and Inner Master steadily ascend, exploring and penetrating each successive level until the height of Sat Lok, the abode of the Lord, is attained. It is here that Sainthood, or God Realization, is bestowed.

So to summarize, the soul is currently entrapped within the human consciousness and does not recognize itself due to the predominance and overpowering nature of the materialistic mind. The nature of all spiritual evolution is based upon emancipating the soul from this very dominion of matter and mind, and thus the soul must gradually begin to collect itself and strive to concentrate its spiritual energies within the third eye. Soul must first negotiate the conscious materialistic mind within the physical consciousness, it must then purify the subconscious mind in the astral plane, and finally, the soul must strip and transcend the unconscious mind located in Trikuti, the second level of Heaven. Having separated itself from the highest mind, referred to as the universal mind, the soul is now able to gain entrance into Daswan Dwar, or the third level of Heaven, and there experience Self Realization for the first time. The heights of Spiritual and God Realization will then follow in sequential order.

This general overview of the divine cosmology within each human being gives adequate definition to the biblical quotes, "The Kingdom of Heaven is within you" and "In my Father's house are many mansions." Likewise, as Buddha stated, "The summit of reality can only be realized within oneself." A great Sufi Master stated, "The source of truth is within, and he himself is the object of his realization." Schopenhauer stated, "The essential to life's happiness resides in what one has in one's Self." And Hazrat Inayat Khan stated, "Verily, it is simpler to find a way to Heaven than to find one's way on earth."

All of these quotes undeniably represent the journey of soul that each individual will ultimately embark upon within one's own precious inner kingdom. Even though most initially wonder how anything so beautiful could possibly be within them, I tell you lovingly and strongly that the human being is the microcosm of the macrocosm, meaning that each individual has an exact duplicate of the outlying universe within oneself. Whatever exists outside, exists inside as well. This great truth is what makes the inner journey of MasterPath, or more precisely, soul's divine journey, so exalted, blissful, and revelatory that it simply must be experienced.

CHAPTER THREE

THE TRUE TEACHINGS

The twenty-first century is seeing the true Teachings
of Light and Sound emerge in America, and this ancient
and direct Path back to Self and God Realization has been
contemporarily coined the MasterPath for two simple reasons. First, the shining goal of all spiritual pursuit is the
attainment of your own Mastership, and second, the means
of accomplishment involves the discovery of the sacred Path
that undeniably lies within your own inner consciousness.
Each and every living being has the sacred Path situated
within them. You are the way, the truth, and the life. For
these reasons, this Divine Teaching is called MasterPath,
for you are the Master and you are the Path. The truth that
you seek is within you, and so too is the Kingdom of Heaven,
as all past and present Masters have unanimously declared.

There are four cardinal principles upon which the
entire spiritual edifice of MasterPath, the true Teachings of
Light and Sound, is established.

1. God the Oversoul: There is one absolute God, and
even though there are over a thousand names for the
Creator, this Divine Being still remains one and the same.
Metaphorically, God can be referred to as the Ocean of
all Consciousness.

2. God's Divine Essence: The divine Essence of God
created the myriad planes, universes, and all that inhabits

and exists within them. This divine Essence of God has been termed by many names such as the Holy Spirit, Word, Logos, Shabda, Nam, and Sound Current. Metaphorically, this divine Essence can be referred to as the creative wave emanating from God, the Ocean of all Consciousness. It is upon this creative wave of the Sound Current that all souls will eventually ascend into their own Self and God Realization.

3. God's Highest Creation: The highest creation in all of God's Kingdom is the individual soul, the divine spark within all living things. The soul is immortal and eternal, and is distinctly independent of body, emotions, and mind. Metaphorically, the soul can be referred to as a drop from the Ocean of all Consciousness, and as such, is imbued with the same attributes and qualities as God, albeit on a miniature scale.

4. The Outer and Inner Masters: The Two Faces of the Master serve in tandem as an emissary or servant of God the Oversoul. The sole objective of the Outer Master is to guide and instruct, but it is the Inner Master who initiates souls into their own Sound Current and escorts them back into Sat Lok. Metaphorically, the Inner Master can be viewed as the Captain of the ship, and His mission is to ferry readied souls across the tumultuous ocean that separates them from their Creator.

MasterPath is an individual spiritual pursuit, which holds that each human being has an indisputable and inherent right to individually worship God and Spirit exclusively within one's own inner temple. While the institutional approach to spiritual attainment is in the majority, insinuating that all humanity shall return to God as a collective whole,

MasterPath clearly breaks from this widely practiced concept and traditional belief. Rather than stressing identification with an institution, an external code of religious rites and ceremonies, or strict adherence to a set code of moral and ethical precepts, once again MasterPath emphasizes the individual relationship exclusively between the soul of the individual and the preeminence of God.

MasterPath is neither a social nor a political organization, nor does it attempt to deny these practices and concepts to others. The soul, in its long and unimaginable course of evolvement throughout the cycles of time, has at one time or another relied upon all differing and varying ways back to the Godhead, even though they have predominantly been externalized and collective approaches. The contemporary understanding of these approaches is that individuals must forfeit their own personal identity for the betterment of the institution. MasterPath does not adopt this widely accepted approach in any manner, for the true Teachings of Light and Sound emphasize the collection and centering of one's energies, not their diffusion, the concentration of one's vital forces, not their scattering into the outside world.

However, MasterPath does not advocate vacating the world and retiring to some remote wilderness or avoiding one's earthly responsibilities. Escapism is not an earmark of the Divine's true Teachings. The true Teachings instruct that it is far more beneficial for the individual to acquire the spiritual talent of transcending the world while presently living within it. By embracing the Divine's Teachings, we are to become better citizens within the culture or nation we find ourselves, a better husband or wife, a more compassionate father or mother, for the soul lovingly exudes and demonstrates its true inner nature in all areas of life. According to MasterPath doctrine, in order to pay proper tribute to truth's inherent nature, we must be conscientious toward ourselves and all others, as the soul is spiritually culpable in all that it does, whether in thought, feeling, or action.

The benefits to be accrued through association with the divine Sound Current are extraordinary. As this purely spiritual Force enters an individual's consciousness, It completely re-orders one's life and brings new levels of self-discipline and harmony into all social, economic, and spiritual conditions. This spiritual Sound lovingly weans the individual from all remaining attachments that have overpowered one, whether through addiction or otherwise, and replaces them with constructive and progressive spiritual realities. Normally, the desires of the mind are unwilling to forfeit any long-standing attachments or pleasures and will staunchly continue this refusal to do so, at least until the mind finds something better with which to replace them. Typically, the mind does not comply with our deepest wishes, and it just cunningly attempts to substitute one pleasure for another. But when the mind begins experiencing the fresh and invigorating currents of the Sound, it becomes enraptured, deeply satisfied, and happily content, and so it begins releasing its white-knuckled grip on all that previously held it prisoner.

Thus, the student's relationships with the entire outside world, with one's own subjective world, one's family, and all external interactions, whether occupational or social, come into a keener balance as one establishes a newer and higher expression of truthful living. The meaning and purpose of life are now clearly presented, and the mysteries which heretofore made little sense become easily decipherable. The conflicts arising between one idea or opinion over another, one chosen faith compared to another, or one political or economic dynamic over another just melt away into oblivion. Fear and uncertainty, pain and heartache, as well as acute misery and incessant despair can no longer hold any valid meaning, and thus they lose their power to disturb or delay the ascending soul.

The binding chains of our fate karma, intent on stripping our entire sense of freedom and liberty, instantly snap at the Inner Master's touch. The apathetic boredom and meaninglessness of our previous existence are miraculously supplanted with a vibrant new reality, which pulsates throughout our inner sense of being and is intent on rising above and conquering all adverse conditions. Our inner spirit effortlessly rises, our perception becomes clear and illuminated, our comprehension becomes broader and deeper than the largest sea, our wavering thoughts find equipoise, and the ever-expanding love and bliss now afforded us bring new levels of peace and tranquility. In short, a complete spiritual metamorphosis visibly transpires, much to the delight of the Light and Sound follower.

MasterPath supports the reality of salvation, not as a reward in the afterlife, but as a spiritual ideal to attain while living. The concept that salvation will be bestowed upon the masses after death is one of the greatest forms of self-deception practiced within the field of religion. Salvation is actually the summum bonum of all spiritual pursuit, and the true Teachings of Light and Sound hold as their supreme objective the task of delivering the soul, in the most direct way, back into the Kingdom of Heaven while we are still living within this mortal coil. The ideal of achieving the Kingdom of Heaven as a reward in the afterlife is not condoned or embraced on the MasterPath, for if this august level of spiritual attainment cannot be experienced while we are living, there is little chance of experiencing it upon our death, or translation from the physical world.

This individual approach back to God does not involve our subjective mind or its companion personality, but only the individual soul within each human being. Soul is the central reality of our composite nature, and only soul can experience true liberation and salvation. MasterPath aims at separating the soul from the confines and limitations of mind and matter, and reuniting the soul with its Source. Soul is a singular drop, while the Creator is the mighty Ocean, and thus the spiritual objective is for the drop to eventually merge back into the depths of its Creator's Ocean once again. MasterPath embraces this spiritual union of soul with its Creator as the supreme objective, and all other ideals must necessarily take a back seat to this incomparable attainment.

As a vessel of the true Teachings, the MasterPath does not proselytize or attempt to manipulate or convert anyone, for it is not concerned with building up its membership or sending emissaries throughout the world. It has no church or temple in the outside world and is free from power plays, coercion, or persuasion of any kind. The decision to investigate or to walk this Path is completely an individual affair. The MasterPath also transcends the social barriers of race, creed, gender, and sexual preference; geographical location and past spiritual training or affiliation do not apply. MasterPath transcends all rites, rituals, and ceremonies, stressing that it is the individual's own personal experience with the incomparable Light and Sound of God which really matters. All worship and devotion are directed toward the spiritual reality within one called Sound, transcending all cultic practice and personality worship entirely.

The call to rediscover one's spiritual roots and divine origin is heard deep within the seeker's own heart, not from the pulpit or from an overly zealous follower of an external faith. It should be clearly understood that MasterPath respects all of the unique endeavors to reunite with the Godhead, whether they are religious, philosophical, or metaphysical in their approaches. Not everyone can follow the same path or its teachings, nor is everyone ready to ascend into the lofty levels of Heaven and attain liberation and salvation within this lifetime. All of the paths in the world simply reflect the multifaceted levels within the Creator's universal body, much like the many grades within the educational system. All are to be seen and understood as having a unique place in the overall unfoldment of the individual soul, and therefore, no one can say this one is right and the other wrong.

The true Teachings of Light and Sound do, however, clearly differentiate between the currents of light and those of Sound, that is, the essential difference between the universal mind power and the spiritual Essence of which soul is comprised. In proper scope and sequence, light comes first in the form of knowledge and illumination, and then the Sound manifests and confers Self and God Realization. This spiritual progression that occurs from light to Sound actually depicts the ascent from divine knowledge to spiritual realization, or the transition from identifying with the mind to realizing the true self in soul. In the view of the Saints, the soul's divine journey back Home is traversed through a series of sequential steps, which can be metaphorically depicted as Jacob's ladder, or the ascending stairway back into Heaven. Therefore, every path and method of devotion that the evolving soul experiences through the march of time has divine purpose and meaning, for each step brings soul closer to the eternal and ultimate goals of Self and God Realization.

As stated previously, this spiritual Teaching of Light and Sound is called the MasterPath, for the truest and purest Path of all resides within your own consciousness, not in the outside world. It is called MasterPath because the attainment of Mastership, or Sainthood, is the highest spiritual ideal that can be attained while living within the human experience. The MasterPath's interest is to assist the student in transcending the ills and woes of karmic experience by rising above mind and matter, affording one a freedom from all binding conditions, whether physical, emotional, or mental. It bestows upon one the lofty qualities of power, love, and wisdom, and graces the soul with the attainments of illumination, enlightenment, and Self, Spirit, and God Realization. Correspondingly, the MasterPath furnishes the means by which the aspirant can surmount all retrogressive tendencies and desires, as well as freeing one from dependence upon any external props or crutches.

MasterPath teaches moderation in all things rather than the rigid and unbending edict of total abstinence, and in this way, the rise in consciousness from the human condition into the spiritual states is accomplished in the most natural way. This ascension in states of consciousness from the lowest to the highest is utterly free of the need for external observances or endless mental reaffirmations. Fasting, strict adherence to ascetic practices, and the performance of difficult asanas, or postures, hold no practical value in the spiritual ascension of soul. Strict moral codes, ceremonies and rites, and rigorous incantations are also considered pointless, for the soul is completely neglected in such practices, meaning that no real and lasting elevation of the spiritual energies can take place.

These above-listed practices, although having relative value to many, do not serve the ultimate objective that a true spiritual seeker aspires to attain. These lower boons and self-imposed disciplines merely serve the means and never the end, for they are, at best, moral recommendations created by human beings. If these aforementioned observances were literally fail-safe, the world at large would be filled with enlightened beings; however, this is the rare exception, and sadly not the norm. No doubt, these moral injunctions and recommendations can pacify the mind and quell certain disturbing emotional reactions, but it is the soul that must be addressed, not simply the body, emotions, or mental states that encumber the soul and diminish its luminosity.

In order to attain the Self and God-realized states, the recommended spiritual discipline must address the indwelling soul and not just the sheaths, or bodies, that cloak and hide the divine being within one. All Saints and Masters have unanimously declared, in uncompromising terms, that the soul is the central reality of the individual. Therefore, without spotlighting or addressing this spiritual entity within oneself, all supposed gain through spiritual practice remains obsolete and the student is actually mis-led. Although very little is known about the soul and its location within the body by the worldly wise, the Masters of Light and Sound do not find these spiritual enigmas to be mysterious at all. To those who are realized, no un-solvable riddle or esoteric mystery exists, nor is there any question that can ever be put to them which is too difficult to answer, for if it were, they could direct one to the prop-er Source.

Once again, the spiritual benefits to be accrued by embracing the true Teachings of Light and Sound are in-numerable and truly unparalleled in scope and stature. So ineffable, incomprehensible, and transcendental are these spiritual gift waves, that only through experiencing them firsthand can any type of comparison be made or mentally envisioned. If pressed to give an analogy of the essential difference between aimlessly wandering in the physical and mental states versus consciously imbibing in the soul state, one need simply compare the state of deep slumber to the wakefulness of daily living.

This spiritual awareness of soul continues to expand exponentially on the Path of Light and Sound until one can eventually embrace the totality of truth. Since the soul is adorned with the divine attributes of power, love, wisdom, and freedom, these wondrous spiritual qualities begin percolating downward into the waking consciousness of the student, bringing untold clarity and newfound revelation. With the love of soul and the Master now constantly present, coupled with the newfound power to control all overt and covert emotional responses, a new equilibrium is developed that effortlessly transcends the anxiety, tension, and nerve-racking conditions of the modern-day world. With the conferring of wisdom, the truth stands before the student unhidden and bare, illusions lose their grip, and in a short while, the mental passions are rendered utterly helpless. All things begin to harmonize, purify, and take on divine meaning as wisdom spreads its wings. The student steadily experiences a new and rejuvenating spiritual freedom – a freedom from an unruly and rebellious mind, a freedom from emotional attachment and all karmic bonds, a freedom from being self-willed, opinionated, and closed-minded, and a freedom from excessive lust, uncontrolled greed, anger, attachment, and vanity. Also included among these gifts is the bestowal of illumination in the astral plane, which is closely followed by complete enlightenment in the mental plane. After the conference of these attainments, the levels of Self, Spirit, and God Realization sequentially manifest, and upon reaching the final stage, one is able to consciously live in the heavenly states of consciousness even while alive in this physical body.

The MasterPath offers the student the most direct and expedient method of re-entering the Kingdom of Heaven, escorting one through all subsequent levels of unfoldment until emancipation and liberation in soul are complete.

Untold gifts and benefits bring constant guidance and protection to one, and upon initiation into the Sound Current, the student's karmic scroll is greatly mitigated, allowing one's deliverance into the ecstatic states of spiritual consciousness to be swift and certain.

The student of a Light and Sound Path comes to cherish the guidance and protection afforded one through the Two Faces of the Master, the Outer and Inner Masters, for one is able to see and hear the Guru on both the inner and outer planes. The Outer Master provides all necessary external instruction, in the form of His living example and through the written and spoken Word, but the Inner Master becomes the aspiring devotee's truest companion and unfailing friend. All possible benefits are accrued through association with the indwelling Master. The Inner Master accompanies the soul through thick and thin, shedding light and love where they would be absent otherwise. He stays with one, not only in life, but at the crossroads of death, greeting the departing soul upon leaving the mortal coil at one's final breath. This eternal Power, called the Inner Master, is both one's silent protector and hidden mentor, and the inexhaustible Source of the higher inspiration required to re-create a new life lived in truth.

A Master Soul comes to reveal our divinity, not to hide it from our view. He comes to release us from the spinning wheel of birth and death, karma and reincarnation, and the overpowering nature of the passions of the mind. He comes to create within us first a love for the soul, and then for the Lord, offering us a road map directly to Its door. He comes to unite us with God the Oversoul, to dispel all ignorance and despair, and to bestow illumination and enlightenment. The true Master deifies our soul, brings hope and great joy, stands by us when no one else will, and He unerringly and lovingly points to the way back Home.

The true Master offers the shortcut to the final solution of God's unsolvable mystery, revealing the Path to soul's ultimate victory, and accompanying us unfailingly along the way until our own spiritual feet are firmly established once again within the heavenly states of consciousness.

The MasterPath student is given a constant infusion of spiritual vigor and renewed strength of spiritual purpose, and above all, one is graced with the opportunity to ultimately take Mastership of one's own life. Once you have experienced the infinite abyss between the small "I" and the large "I" within yourself, once you have seen the true distinction between the false self and the real self, this realization can never be taken from you. The benefits and gift waves that automatically manifest in the student's consciousness are truly too numerous to list, and proper credit could never be given them through the medium of paper and ink.

Thus, all Masters of the Light and Sound leave the final assessment to the individual soul and one's own first-hand experience. The Saints lovingly say: Rise to the eye focus and survey the spiritual landscape from there. If what you see is not to your liking, then your observations and judgments can be considered fair.

CHAPTER FOUR

THE TRUE MASTER

Those spiritual seekers who truly yearn for the liberation and salvation of their souls; those who have witnessed the plight of the human condition, and thus desire only to transcend the woes and ills within this materialistic prison house; those who have escaped the confines of the mental labyrinth of theological hairsplitting, and now desire only a clear and lucid description of the shining Path leading to the Creator's door…need only familiarize themselves with the incomparable and revelatory nature of the Light and Sound Teachings.

In order to actually attain the lofty pinnacles of Self and God Realization, thereby exposing the physical and mental senses for the imposters that they are, as well as deftly rising above the incessant play of the desires and passions of the mind that afflict all of humankind…a perfected and fully realized Master is all that is ever required.

The spiritual assistance afforded the soul through the divine auspices of a commissioned Living Master cannot be adequately conveyed to the struggling spirit, one who wishes only for peace and tranquility in a world flooded with mental anxiety and spiritual discord. However, the individual mind, oversaturated with impressions of deceit and fraudulent misrepresentation, finds it difficult to believe and trust in anyone within this present day and age.

Thus, no spiritual dilemma is more poignant and heart-wrenching than that of a yearning soul who is duly prepared and ready for the spiritual ascent, and yet, has been unable to set anchor in the harbor of truth. Cast upon the ocean of empirical existence without compass or sail, such a soul remains void of precise bearings and is incessantly tossed about by the gale-like winds of the physical and mental forces. To quiet these torrential storms, once again bringing peace and tranquility to what has otherwise been a ceaseless barrage of tumultuous waves and strong rip currents within the seeker's inner consciousness, is the divine mission of the Master and the celestial Sound which accompanies Him. Without this tandem of divine intervention, as well as the Creator's resurrecting power of truth and love, the individual soul is utterly helpless and risks forever being lost at sea.

The Lord's promise to each and every one of Its children is that once this divine connection to the Master and Sound has been re-established, the soul will never again be left without full-blown sails to escort its ship, nor will it be absent an experienced Captain to safely ferry its vessel across the perilous ocean of existence now separating it from its Creator. There is a fail-safe passageway and a secret, hidden door…a river of divine elixir, and a golden compass that can magnetically direct soul along the way, but the Divine Creator has granted their possession only to the perfected Saints, the true and bona fide Masters of the Teachings of Light and Sound.

These Godly Souls come not to imprison the infant soul, but to free it. They come not to divide, but to reunite the soul with its long-lost Source. The Masters have no interest in revitalizing the religious order of the times, for their primary concern involves only the emancipation of the indwelling soul. They come not to form a fresh religion or to establish a contemporary new creed, but only to resurrect the inner pathway, teaching ceaselessly the eternal principles leading to the Creator's door. They care little for the teeming masses and the materialistic values they purport, but will invest all of their divinity to assist those individuals who desire to embark on their own unique quest for life's ultimate goals of Self and God Realization. The Masters covet not the possessions and wealth of others, for they wish only to quietly bestow upon the readied few their own abundant riches in consciousness. Their divine bounty is immeasurable, for all that they possess has come not from themselves, but directly from the Divine, and they serve only as the humble dispensers of God's gracious mercy and infinite love. The Lord stands as the Eternal Giver, having no interest in receiving, and so too do the Saints and Masters who live in the dungeons of the lower worlds as shining beacons and loving extensions of God's infinite mercy and grace.

Contrary to religious myth, these Sons of God do not experience a virgin birth, for they enter the world like any other human being, nor do they drop from the sky fully endowed with all of the divine attributes, loudly proclaiming their wares and miraculous spiritual powers. In truth, the Saints embody a pure and surprisingly quiet humility, born from their own negotiation of soul's wondrous spiritual journey, which all others too will eventually be graced the opportunity to embrace. The Masters' greatness is due only to their completion of the extensive spiritual training that has equipped them in their divine appointment to assist others in need. In the fullness of time, all souls will ultimately serve in this divine capacity as well, for when a soul's exit from the lower worlds is complete, one's own spiritual mission is then lovingly revealed. Thus, the Masters never project an attitude of being "holier than thou," more often than not placing themselves beneath the lowly status of a servant. In the eyes of all

Masters, there is nothing greater than service to the Lord's divine will.

The Masters pointedly convey that the entire spiritual journey transpires in soul's consciousness, requiring one to travel no further than the region between the third eye aperture and the crown of the human head. The sensory-intellectual consciousness, that is, the everyday conscious mind, exists and expresses itself beneath the third eye, while in contrast, the transcendental, spiritual conscious-ness of soul springs into expression just above this third eye focus. The Masters reveal that the entire creation of God is uniquely reflected within the human's own physical frame, spanning all the way from the soles of one's feet to the top of the head. All of the nine regions within the macrocosm, or the Creator's universal body, are micro-cosmically contained within the human's physical body as well. Consequently, all spiritual ascension, along with the inner movement of consciousness throughout the en-tire spiritual journey, transpires nowhere other than within the physical body and the cavity of the human brain. Therefore, all efforts to mentally or astrally project into the realms of the psychic worlds are shunned by all Light and Sound Masters, for the soul need only travel within its own bodily structure and explore the innate wonders of its own microcosmic universe.

It is imperative that the sincere seeker of truth under-stands the importance of awakening the slumbering soul within, for the soul is not in control prior to this awaken-ing, and thus it is the emotional and mental senses which initially lead the seeker's spiritual search. Many seekers, despite their best intentions, attempt to live the spiritual life according to the dictates of their own individual minds and, as a result, are only able to enliven or further develop a more refined mental state of consciousness, or some intellectual ideal of what spirituality should embody. This is one reason why a Master is so essential, for it is only natural to follow one's own mental inclinations. However, without the counsel of a true Master, these very mental tendencies continue to captivate the soul, holding it prisoner indefinitely within the web of mental theory and the maze of intellectualism.

If objectively and dispassionately observed, it is quite clear that the major religions of the world rely upon a host of ascended Masters. Although this may be beneficial in providing a relative degree of evolvement for the mind, it is wholly insufficient in the eyes of the Masters, because it is extremely difficult to believe and have faith in something you have never seen. When the ascended Masters completed their divine missions, they left this theater of action and transferred their responsibilities of redeeming souls to those succeeding them. Thus, in a scenario such as we see in the major religions today, the true role and purpose of a Living Master has been reduced to a vague image, a fleeting spiritual impulse, and a formless figure from the distant past.

One's chosen Master, ideally, should embody both an Outer and Inner Form, for how could a devotee even be properly initiated absent the Master's presence in the physical realm? How could the imperceptible nature of God be perceived or even related to except through the consciousness of the Master and His living example on this earthly plane of action? When the Masters of Light and Sound speak of the Two Faces of the Master, they are referring to an elite line of Guruship that only the true Saints can possess. To be visibly manifest on the physical plane, while simultaneously being able to assume form and manifest on the inner planes of the student's consciousness, is the divine boon of Anami's true Saints. This is what vastly accelerates the expansion of consciousness on the Light and Sound Path and literally sling-shots the indwelling soul to unimaginable heights.

The Outer Master can physically teach and guide, but it is the transcendent Inner Master who carries us Home. The outer form of the Master is presently here on this physical plane, but the Inner Master is our constant companion and guide throughout the entire spiritual journey. The Inner Master takes divine form on each successive level of Heaven only to assist and deliver the ascending soul, remaining with the spiritual entity until the final goal is won. It is the resplendent Inner Master who awaits His devoted chelas at the time of death when the soul leaves the mortal coil; it is He who then takes charge of the soul, trumping and superseding both the messengers of death and Dharam Rai, the lord and final judge of the dead.

Thus, to have as your chosen Guru one who can truly embody the two forms of the Master is the highest and most sublime spiritual assistance offered humankind. With both the Outer and Inner Master at one's side, the student increasingly perceives truth through one's own physical, mental, and spiritual senses, intensifying the stunning reality of this divine journey and fast-forwarding the soul into new and more rarefied states of consciousness.

The Teachings of the Light and Sound doctrine are so vast in scope that one can easily study a lifetime and still not fully fathom their depths. Such being the case, what the aspiring seeker really needs is true sincerity, true purpose, and true humility. If you desire a higher level of spiritual truth, it is there for the taking, and you need only go inside your own sacred temple to find it. However, you will need a true Guide. You will need a special someone who has traversed this spiritual journey before, someone who can expertly guide you, illuminating the way and protecting you through the perilous and unseen dangers of the inner psychic worlds.

It can be very difficult to convey in comprehensible terms the value and reach of the true Master's great love, His constant counsel and guidance, and the clarity of vision that this Power spontaneously resurrects within the seeker's heart of hearts. Nowhere is this made more clear than in the personal experience of the ascending soul. As countless devotees have attested, the Master's reach extends far beyond the seven seas and spans across the largest galaxy imaginable to humankind. The infinite abyss between the Creator and the creation, the unknown chasm between the soul and mind, and the unsolvable mystery between truth and untruth instantly dissolve with just a touch of the Inner Master's hand. With His touch, all secrets are disclosed, all riddles are removed, and the esoteric interpretation of all sacred scripture becomes easily decipherable. The mind's angst is laid to rest, its bewilderment and perplexity are supplanted with clarity of vision, and the emptiness of mundane existence is filled with divine purpose and vital meaning.

The Master's divine treasure chest, bearing the gifts of rapturous bliss, overwhelming love, and untainted mercy, is opened wide to all who wish to follow, simply flooding the spiritual senses of those who choose to imbibe in this incomparable divine elixir. The advent of the Master within the inner sanctum of the spiritual pilgrim's heart cannot be described, but is readily visible in the swelling tears of a devotee whose tongue is helplessly tied in silence. To be considered one of His own, to hear His melodious voice despite the confusion and clamor of the world, and to sense His loving touch when all else is cold and distant bring fresh inspiration and a wondrous new vitality to the soul caged within the body consciousness. When armed with the Master's uncanny benevolence and secretly defended by

His unerring protection and guardianship, the slumbering soul begins to awaken, and this commences the wondrous return journey of soul back to its primordial Homeland.

Although wonderstruck initially, the infant soul begins to adapt to the powerful spiritual inflows that are descending upon it and is enraptured beyond description at each and every ascending level, just happy to have come so far. Even when entrapped within the consciousness of the body, the soul always knew that God was inconceivably great, but never did it have an inkling of just how all-encompassing God's greatness could be. It was told that God had previously donned the garb of man and manifested His divine Essence upon this planet, but was unaware of this miracle in present time. It had heard of saintly Souls in times past, but never dreamed it would one day include itself among them. Soul had come to believe that the Source of truth was unavailable, deeply hidden within the halls of some remote monastery or secret cavern in the distant mountain wilderness, but certainly not enshrined within the folds of its own innermost consciousness. Thus, in quiet wonder, the realized soul will unhesitatingly proclaim that the exact point at which the true Master glanced its way was indeed the most pivotal and profound moment within its entire existence.

CHAPTER FIVE

THE TRUE SOUND CURRENT

With the gift of the true Teachings, the true Path is revealed and the overall purpose of an individual's life is made crystal clear. And with the advent of a true Master, humankind is given a living example, someone who can light the way and confer the spark of inspiration needed to rekindle the fires of true spirituality. But it is truly the bestowal of Sound, the majestic and peerless Essence of God, which allows the consciousness to rise upward, easily transcending the temporal and transitory nature of matter and mind, while simultaneously resurrecting the shining divinity of soul. It is the celestial Sound Current that all souls seek, for upon Its wondrous power of upliftment does the soul become revitalized, divinely re-energized, and ultimately made fit to enter its long-forgotten Home.

Upon the wings of this enchanting Melody does the soul first glimpse itself, and it is awestruck by its own divine nature. The soul, supported by this river of super-consciousness, enthusiastically takes each successive step until it finally enters into its own sublimity and anticipated Godhood. The Sound Current is the melodious Voice of God, which constantly speaks words of love and wisdom to the ear of soul, beckoning continuously for soul to heed Its call. It can be heard in the stillness of the night sweetly conveying that one is not alone, nor has one been forgotten. This rapturous Sound belongs to all of humankind, for It is the soul's divine inheritance. The Sound reposes Itself within the hidden temple of the body, just waiting for soul's recognition of It when It becomes visible and audible upon the Inner Master's sacred touch.

The Sound Current's sole objective is to arouse the infant soul from its age-old slumber, restoring its reason to be and live once again, in spite of the untold heartache and misery of its lifetimes lived in the past. The Sound empowers the soul and washes it clean, restoring the brilliance of illumination and enlightenment within its spiritual senses. It is upon this heavenly Sound that the traveling soul ascends, entering, mastering, and transcending each region until the Court of the Lord is gloriously encountered and made manifest to the soul once again.

The purity of Sound cleanses the vessel, removing the stain of all karmic burdens. The Sound empties the chalice of illusion, refilling it to the brim until it spills over with the incandescent nature of truth. This ineffable Sound beckons the soul to drink, and soul becomes intoxicated with Its divine elixir. The ambrosia of Sound entrances the soul, bringing to it all that was missing, all that is needed, as It quenches the thirsty and parched soul with Its replenishing and vital Essence. With the light of this Current's vision and the Sound of Its voice, the soul gains heavenly sight and wanders no more. It is this Sound, and only this Sound, that can deliver the soul into its own realization, ultimately conferring all of the coveted qualities and attributes of Sainthood.

The Sound Current is God's eternal gift to the soul, and It is reactivated exclusively through the agency of the Living Master. The Sound is a river of grace, bliss, and mercy flowing from the Almighty to all regions below, and upon this stream of His eternal Essence does the soul rise to love, liberty, and freedom once again. The Sound is the Essence of all essences, the pearl of great price, and It bestows untold wealth within the vitals of soul. It is the outpouring of God's unlimited power and love, representing all that the Divine Creator is, both manifested and unmanifested alike.

This magnificent Spirit of God is omnipresent, omnipotent, and omniscient, and It is the alpha and omega of all existing creation. All of the lords within each respective region, plane, and subplane, as well as the spiritual powers entrusted to them, owe their missions and existence to this one, indisputable river of Light and Sound. All life is sustained by Its greatness, all planets and constellations hang by Its power, and all of the levels of Heaven gain support from and are inextricably infused with the Sound Current's infinite energy. The Sound is literally the Life Force Itself.

The origin from which this majestic Sound Current issues forth is the mighty throne of Anami, the Supreme Deity who dwells within the nameless, formless, and inaccessible realm termed Anami Lok. It was the stirring of Anami's divine will that gave rise to this creative desire to project Itself downward and outward into what was once an empty void of space and nothingness. Into this infinite vacuum of nonexistence did Lord Anami project Its very Essence, first creating the realm of Agam Lok, followed in succession by Alakh Lok and Sat Lok. This very Essence, this inconceivable wave of creative Power, is termed the divine Sound Current, or the eternal Spirit of Anami's holy and infinite Beingness. These higher realms of Anami's creation are purely spiritual regions, which can only be traversed and inhabited by the Saints and Masters, as well as those disciples who have completed the spiritual journey.

From Sat Lok, which is considered the fifth realm of Heaven, did this incandescent river of Sound then descend even further, diffusing and diluting Its effulgent Essence with each descending plane of creation. In this devolutional cycle, Bhanwar Gupha was created, the realm of soul's true spiritual Essence, and this was then followed by Daswan Dwar, the realm of Self Realization. Next came Trikuti, the home of the universal mind power, followed by the realm of the astral worlds, within which light is the primary quality. And finally, the pinda, or earth, plane came into reflective existence, and the individual mind was created to oversee the human being. Upon each of these multiple levels of creation, an overlord was then placed to regulate and supervise the spiritual responsibilities inherent to each respective plane.

Our own Mother Earth is considered a mere infinitesimal grain of sand within the scope and breadth of the entire physical universe. The physical universe extends as far as the naked eye can see and beyond the depths which the strongest telescope can penetrate; it incorporates not only our own unique planet and solar system, but all constellations and our own Milky Way, along with the billions of other outlying galaxies intermittently dotting the vastness of infinite space. Our physical universe is not static, but is dynamically pulsating and ever-expanding at the speed of light, enlarging itself with every nanosecond.

Yet, in the same breath, the entire physical universe can be described as only a tiny and nearly insignificant speck when compared to the expansive realms directly above it. Thus, it is utterly futile for the mental senses to attempt to fully encompass the infinite panorama of all nine regions within Anami's created universe, for even the unrestrained imagination fails miserably when trying to grasp its staggering magnitude. Only a divine Power capable of creating such a kaleidoscopic array of variegated life forms could be employed to form and sustain these mighty realms of existence and all that inhabits them, and this is what the Masters term the almighty Sound Current.

This same eternal Sound Current resides latent within the consciousness of all humankind, just above and behind the two eyes, and this very Current comes into dynamic expression when any individual adopts the Living Master's divine tutelage and is initiated by Him. The Sound Current of God is literally the heartbeat of both humankind and the outlying created universe, and all things therefore owe their existence to this preeminent Power. Over incomprehensible periods of time, this gigantic, creative Wave slowly recedes from the heart of Anami, and then It steadily retreats back again to Its Source. In other words, the outward, centrifugal movement of this Current reverses its motion in the fullness of time, and It then becomes the centripetal power, which returns to Its original Source. On the outward flow of this Current all life is created, as teeming multitudes of souls devolve into the lower kingdoms, but upon Its return, or inward movement, all souls ascend, evolving step by step as they are magnetically drawn back to the bosom of the Creator. The connection to this ascending and evolving Current of Sound is what the Masters re-awaken within their disciples, and this explains, in part, why the ascent in consciousness on the MasterPath is so distinctly accelerated, at least when compared or held in contrast to the relative attainments possible within the twenty-first century's light paths.

It is this resounding Sound Current that serves as the sole connecting link between God and humankind. As previously stated, the Sound reposes Itself and lies latent within the third eye aperture, which is the headquarters for soul and mind within the human frame. Both the mind and the soul are inextricably locked together within this plexus, neither one being wholly free or independent of the other. In fact, in the human condition, the physical, conscious mind has dominance over the slumbering soul. Therefore, in the beginning of the spiritual journey, pointed emphasis is given to releasing the iron grip the mental senses have over the spiritual senses of soul. The soul, being forced to abide in enemy territory, finds itself overpowered by the mental forces and must, through necessity, acquiesce to the conscious and subconscious minds of the individual. To reverse this condition and facilitate the re-awakening of soul, this Sound Current situated in the third eye must be reactivated, which visibly serves to rebalance the scales in soul's favor. It is the initiation from a genuine Sat Guru, or true Master, which brings into kinetic expression this once latent and dormant Sound Current, and upon Its re-awakening, the spiritual saga of soul's divine journey commences.

The simple reason why most humans are unaware of this innate Sound Current that silently exists within their very own consciousness is that the Sound Current cannot descend beneath the third eye focus, and so It is unable to percolate downward into their conscious minds for easy recognition. On the contrary, the attention, which is scattered throughout the body and the outside world, must be regathered in order to rise upward to the third eye where conscious contact with this innate Sound Current can be made once again. This is why the teachings of conventional religion, as well as the intelligence of humankind, have no concept or workable insight into this cosmological powerhouse of pure, unadulterated spirituality. Therefore, the salient wisdom to be drawn from this necessary stage of self-imposed ignorance is that the soul must willingly agree to the spiritual ascension, for by doing so, it inevitably elevates its position from the human to the spiritual consciousness, which in turn introduces soul to its own inner Sound Current.

Thus, with soul's agreement, coupled with the Living Master and His initiation, the soul is ushered into the orbit of this wondrous Sound Current. The soul then strives to merge itself into this mighty river of Light and Sound, learning to release all of its cares and concerns, its dreams and unfulfilled promises. And in return, this mighty Current of Sound, which is now rebounding and evolving back toward the heart of God, carries the soul upon Its returning centripetal wave directly into the heavenly states of consciousness.

The Living Masters have been appointed as the Spiritual Custodians and Divine Pourers of this incomprehensible Stream of Anami's living consciousness. There are simply no carefully chosen words that can be pressed into the most comprehensible phrases, no matter how well-intended, which can possibly give proper form or fully encompass the indescribable, imperceptible, and utterly majestic nature of Anami's Essence. It is solely through the sacrament of initiation that this blessed Sound is conferred upon the soul as a supreme gift from our Almighty Creator, and this divine gift clearly saves the day, It saves our life, and so too does It grant salvation to our indwelling soul.

CHAPTER SIX

DISCLOSURE OF A HIDDEN SECRET

After being exposed to the concepts and ideas of twenty-first century spirituality, many evolved souls are easily perceiving the overwhelming discrepancies and glaring inconsistencies within the conventional messages coming not only from the pulpits, but also from the overly zealous antics of those who follow the numerous religious doctrines in existence today. Unfavorable impressions are sure to follow such unsettling observations, and a sense of disdain, or even an open aversion to all things spiritual, can take root within the perceptual consciousness of these individuals. Many times, these same individuals are simultaneously seeking the higher consciousness, but they remain innocently unaware that this very quest actually qualifies them as seekers of truth. This is understandable, for these special few seek a level of truth that is wholly unknown and completely unrecognizable to the status quo of the collective consciousness.

These forgotten seekers living on the fringe of society's norms, and also on the periphery of traditional spiritual approaches, will oftentimes subconsciously recoil when any reference is made to the conventional terms of religion or spirituality. Comparatively speaking, their own individual mindsets are more tempered toward endeavors that involve self-discovery, or the realization of the self, than they are toward any message that is overspilling with religious or spiritual overtones. This particular point of view is encountered more frequently than not in contemporary times. Thus, I would like to explain, in part, why perhaps so many of these individuals have turned a deaf ear and are now viewing the true quest for the higher consciousness as something completely different than what modern-day religions or conventional spiritual paths are offering.

The class of religious devotees who have embraced the traditional constructs are basically attempting to establish a personal relationship with their idea of God prior to realizing their own truest self. While this is highly noble and even necessary, their concept of God still remains within the orbit of the universal mind power, which is housed in the second level of Heaven termed Trikuti, the region in which lord Brahm serves as the presiding deity. Brahm is believed to be the supreme Lord God within all contemporary religions, although the Masters of the Light and Sound respectfully draw a distinct line between Brahm, the presiding deity of the second level of Heaven, and Anami, the presiding Deity of the eighth level of Heaven. Brahm is the lord of the mind, while Anami is the Lord of the soul.

In actuality, the pursuit of the higher consciousness is a far more evolved approach than is devotion to or worship of the lord Brahm and his essence, which is termed the universal mind power. Subsequently, the conclusions of the "forgotten seekers" who were previously referred to are correct, for they have intuitively sensed that the traditional religious and spiritual approaches available to them do not offer the highest means of true expansion in consciousness, especially if Self Realization is the envisioned goal. Likewise, it is a self-evident truth to all past and present Masters that no one has ever attained Self Realization by scrupulously adhering to Brahm's religious or metaphysical edicts.

Therefore, a brief overview of lord Brahm becomes necessary, for this negative overlord desires only to obscure the innate divinity of soul, and he does so largely through the widely accepted belief that he is the ultimate Lord God who should receive our exclusive worship. Actually, the lord Brahm is the father of many, not of the One which all Saints extol. Lord Brahm is the universal weaver of all illusion, delusion, and deceit. He is the sovereign lord of light, but with light come shadows. Lord Brahm's chief duty is to conceal the indwelling soul from our sight, and so in its place, he has erected the lower three minds, suggesting that their illusory identifications are the end-all and be-all of all spiritual pursuit. Brahm's essence, called the universal mind power, creates, sustains, and destroys all creation from Trikuti on downward, and so the greatness of his power in these regions is visibly manifest, although he has literally no power whatsoever within the true spiritual regions situated just above.

Brahm's gifts are always framed within the limitations of the intellectual senses, such as divine knowledge, realization of the universal mind, and its corresponding attainment of cosmic consciousness. Lord Brahm relentlessly strives to keep the soul prisoner within his kingdom, and he ruthlessly uses karma and reincarnation as his primary weapons. Brahm has cleverly created all of the divergent light paths ever known to humankind, and each one ultimately leads back to his realm. He is the dispenser of all justice, and he supervises the law of karma well. His divine mission has been to take the one, indivisible Current of Sound descending from above and to dissect It, introducing polar opposites to all that exists in his dual creation. His duties entail keeping a workable balance in the lower three worlds, and thus he periodically sends prophets, sages, and other lower incarnations to uplift and instill positivity and well-being within these realms once again. However, this balance is always restored within the dualistic parameters of right and wrong, good and bad, or virtuous and non-virtuous, which can only simulate and reflect true spirituality, but are not actually a part of it.

The extent of Brahm's responsibilities is nearly incomprehensible, but nevertheless, his rule extends only through the realm of Trikuti, that is, the second level of Heaven. Brahm's splendor and range of rule should never be questioned, but only understood, for all of Brahm's power and authority have been relegated to him by Anami, Lord of the eighth spiritual region. The students of the Living Master have set their goals far higher than Brahm and his chief agent, the mind, and so they view lord Brahm's entrusted responsibility to create, sustain, and supervise the lower three worlds as merely one of the many subordinate positions within Anami's overall hierarchy. Again, lord Brahm created the mind, and the Divine Anami created the soul. Just as the soul is an extension of Lord Anami and Its fountainhead of Sound, so too is the mind an exact replica of lord Brahm and his essence, the universal mind power. Brahm's spiritual power, as great as it is, cannot create or destroy a soul, nor can lord Brahm ever redeem a soul. He can, however, redeem the mind, and this is why the power of his illusion is so great. Just as the soul wishes to merge with its original Source, so too does the mind. Brahm created the mind, and so in the view of the mind, Brahm is the ultimate source, and this is why many mistakenly believe that the spiritual journey has ended when the mind merges back into its original source. However, do not expect Brahm to disclose this grand illusion.

On the contrary, Brahm executes his power and rule by imposing the edicts of karma and reincarnation upon his chief agent, which is the individual human mind. Both the inexorable law of cause and effect, as well as the endless cycles of birth and death, hang mercilessly around the necks of all living beings and allow no possible means of escape. The individual mind is mechanical in nature, and so it blindly follows whatever moral and ethical precepts are defined by Brahm, king of the dual worlds. Brahm's inherent duality then infiltrates the individual's own code of conduct, which results in the unity of truth being relegated to the opposite poles of positivity and negativity, good and bad, or virtue and sin.

It is a well-known fact among all Saints that these basic and well-intended guidelines, or moral premises, simply fall into the parameters of good and bad karma. Brahm's promise is that good karma will create a heavenly paradise, while bad karma will incur hell or levels of purgatory. But what Brahm does not tell you is what the Saints and Masters lovingly wish to reveal – in either scenario, whether a visit to paradise or an excursion through hell, upon its completion, the soul will again be required to reincarnate back into this physical plane. This is why even angels, devas, and heavenly spirits pine for the human incarnation, for they have been imprisoned within their wealth of good karma, requiring that they first expend this karma before they too must reincarnate back into the physical world once again.

The Masters unequivocally state that good karmas alone are not sufficient to redeem the soul. Bad karmas are clearly iron shackles, but good karmas are merely golden chains, and neither does anything other than adorn the mind in its incessant fight between good and evil. Brahm's greatest spell of deceit is his unscrupulous monopoly of our worship, for his primary mission is to cast the illusion that he is the Almighty God, not our own indwelling soul or the Divine Anami. If such illusive tactics are accepted as genuine truth, the sons and daughters of humanity can never discover that they are actually the sons and daughters of God.

In this sense, true spirituality has been hijacked, for the mind now worships Brahm as the ultimate Lord, and similarly, it views the universal mind power as the true Spirit. The mind can become so overly enamored with the worship of Brahm that it completely forgets about the quest for the self, the soul, and the true spiritual consciousness. Consequently, all character development is stymied and only lateral growth is possible, for the mind assumes it has been saved or liberated, and consciously halts its search for the higher truth. All of this is to the glory of the mind and Brahm, but to the utter defeat of soul and its quest to uncover its own divinity. All truth seekers must eventually come to realize that God is housed within them, not embodied in some externally deified form or enshrined in an outside temple.

The individual's realization of one's own divinity is the primary intent of the Teachings of MasterPath, for as a truth seeker, you are not looking for another's spirituality, but only your own. Thus, there is a little story of old I would like to share in the hopes that it will more clearly convey this great truth.

THE FABLE OF THE PRAYING DOG

This is Zero's story. He is reputed to be the largest dog in the world. Among the things he does is go through the motions of prayer. On pious knees he prostrates himself and covers his face with sanctimonious paws. It is related that one day Zero was questioned as such:

"Zero, to what church do you belong?" he was asked. Zero appeared not to understand and exclaimed, "Church! What's church?" "Church," he was answered, "is a place where people go to pray. God is in the church." "Well, I never heard of that," Zero replied. "The God I know about is in people. When I see a gentle face I say, 'This is God,' and I look up to it and worship it. When a kind hand strokes me, I say, 'This is the hand of God.' When a child embraces me, I feel the loving kindness of God."

But whoever was questioning the dog could not understand this, for he had always believed God was only in the church. And so he said to the dog, "I never heard of that before." "You are like me," the dog observed, "I never heard of God in the church, and you never heard of God in people." And the man replied, "Is He in all people, in atheists, for example?" And the dog replied, "Once an atheist was good to me. He scratched my back for me and held his arm about my neck. And I said, 'This is God,' and I looked up to him and worshiped him." "And what do you pray for when you pray?" the man asked the dog. "I pray that God shall always be in all men," the dog answered. "God is the goodness of men by which I live."

But the man could not understand the religion of the dog and went about saying, "The dog has a strange religion. He sees God in men, but of course, he is a dumb animal and can't be expected to have an enlightened religion." And the man went to the church to seek God.

Zero walked to the shade of a tree and lay down, amazed that he knew the God in man better than the man did himself. And while scratching his head, Zero wondered how it was that God went to the church to find himself.

～◯

Worship the gods if you must, but according to the Saints and Masters, this external form of worship is simply an illusory imitation, a pale reflection of true spirituality. True spirituality involves the discovery of soul as the central reality of one's own beingness, and once this consciousness of soul is discovered and given birth, it becomes the sole reality which should then be evolved, expanded, and fully realized. Therefore, from the lofty viewpoint of the Saints, it is not the individual followers, but lord Brahm, who has been the hidden culprit and silent instigator of all visible dissension and observable discrepancies within the frame-work of the world's religions. This spiritual enigma between one religion and another, between Brahm and Lord Anami, and similarly between the mind and soul, is what creates the seeker's dilemma. This spiritual riddle is nearly indecipherable as long as the seeker remains in the mind's sensory-intellectual consciousness, but when the consciousness of soul is given birth, this same enigma resolves itself instantly.

The Masters of Light and Sound distinctly point out that the divine purpose behind all of creation is not to worship the karmic lord, but to gradually evolve the soul's consciousness from the lesser to the greater, from the light to the Sound, until that time when the soul aspires to its own Self and Godhood. The evolution of soul's consciousness takes place over vast periods of time, giving rise to such terms as millennia, ages, and yugas, all of which have been created to help measure the duration of the cycles of time.

Contrary to popular belief, the human being does not have a monopoly on the indwelling soul, nor does the soul inhabit only the human body, for the soul has inhabited many different life forms in its long evolutionary journey. The evolution of consciousness extends from the atom into the plant, animal, and human kingdoms, and the human being represents the height of creation. Thus, the human has been given the responsibility of ultimately transitioning from the human consciousness into the spiritual consciousness, and many lifetimes are afforded the soul in order to accomplish this ascension. This is why the human experience is so coveted by the lower life forms, for only in the human incarnation can the soul finally realize its true self and gain entry back into the heavenly states of consciousness. This brief description offers an overview of the vast cycle of soul's conscious evolution and the encounters it must negotiate with its own mind and lord Brahm, the completion of which is termed God Realization by the Saints.

In order to facilitate this grand transition from the human consciousness to the spiritual consciousness, the Masters emphasize the shining reality of the Sound Current, for it is this spiritual Power alone which is able to transport the soul back into the heavenly Kingdom. The power of the light, or the universal mind power, has accompanied soul's evolution from the very beginning and, in fact, has contributed greatly to it. However, the height of mind's reach extends only to Trikuti, and there the mission of the light currents comes to an end. From this point upward, the higher Current of Sound must be relied upon to finish the remainder of the soul's journey, for light can help the soul attain the mental realms of Trikuti, but it is only the celestial Sound which can escort the soul into Sat Lok, the ultimate Home of truth.

To recapitulate, lord Brahm is the presiding deity of the mind, and he supervises the dualistic nature of all life, both positive and negative. He represents these forces of positive and negative, good and evil, which are called God and Satan in traditional religious terminology. Lord Brahm's role is two-fold. His positive duty is to prepare and evolve both the spiritual entity and the mind through successive incarnations, rewarding the entity with good karma if one's actions have been progressive, and levying bad karma against the entity if one's actions have been retrogressive. The acquisition of both good and bad karma remains strictly relative to the mind alone. In this way, the tandem of mind and soul gradually evolve based specifically on one's own actions, both good and bad. Eventually, the spiritual entity becomes prepared to embrace the inner Path and to leave the counsel of mind and Brahm completely.

The negative aspect of Brahm involves his herculean efforts to conceal the soul, insisting that the individual entity is only a mind, that nothing greater exists than Brahm himself, and that all worship should therefore be relegated and directed to him, and him alone. This encapsulates Brahm's hidden secret, and he unscrupulously uses this grand illusion as a power play over the indwelling soul.

Lord Brahm is not allowed to let any soul leave his kingdom until that soul is fully prepared to embrace the higher and more refined spiritual realities that exist above his realm. Thus, he uses the powers of karma, reincarnation, illusion, and maya to hold the soul prisoner within his kingdom, which extends from the physical plane up through the second level of Heaven, termed Trikuti.

Lord Brahm, or the traditional "God" to all of humankind, is the supreme ruler to all below him. His magnificence cannot be questioned, only his motive. Even though the Masters of Light and Sound respect his mission and relate to it as being absolutely necessary, they do not agree with Brahm's basic premise, which is to say, the mind is not the true self, nor is the universal mind power the pure essence of truth and Anami. Brahm's closely guarded secret is that he is not revealing or disclosing the fact that higher and more sublime spiritual regions exist above his realm of rule. Brahm openly claims that there are no Gods above him, but when the soul does enter these regions just above Brahm's relative reign, this universal illusion and the false rule of mind are forever shattered. Only upon meeting the present Living Master and discovering one's own inner Path, followed by establishing a relationship between soul and the Sound Current, can one escape this endless cycle of birth and death, the law of karma, and the antics of mind and its deity, lord Brahm.

And so, the colossal illusion that lord Brahm weaves for the soul is that neither God nor truth resides within the individual, but in temples, churches, and ashrams, and therefore, all worship should be exclusively placed in him rather than in the innate divinity of soul. This illusion can be illustrated by a boy of five or six years old innocently assuming that in order to have a child, he need only pray to God, and it shall be done. In the absence of personal experience, the boy would have no other recourse but to think this way, but in truth, only when he reaches adulthood and employs his own powers of procreation will a child be born. Similarly, Brahm cannot just bestow our own inner child upon us, even though he implies he can, for the soul must employ the power of its own inherent divinity to ultimately birth the child of true spirituality.

Thus, in the view of the Light and Sound Masters, it is paramount for the student of truth to seek the counsel and assistance of a Living Master, that is, if Self and God Realization are your cherished goals. If these illustrious attainments are not your spiritual objective, then it matters little what your belief of choice may be. But for those aspiring toward liberation and emancipation, the value of a Living Master is irreplaceable, for only through the escort of a true and genuine Master can the fledgling soul gain entry into its own spiritual regions.

The recommended procedure is to grab hold of the robe of the Living Master, striving not only to be schooled in the letter of truth, but in the Spirit of truth as well. Upon rending the veil over the third eye and untying the knotted condition of mind and soul, our spirit enters the temple within and beholds the Inner Master, who then lovingly confers the Sound Current upon the new arrival. Since both the soul and the Sound are of the same essence, their attraction is mutual and magnetic. The Sound, formerly lying dormant, now begins to dynamically express Itself, which changes the entire course of events for the individual entity. Step by step, the soul merges itself into this celestial Sound, moving steadily inward and upward until the borders of Sat Lok are attained.

Seekers are not advised to attempt this divine journey on their own, for if they do, their own minds become their masters. It is also inadvisable to attempt the ascent through the auspices of a deceased Master, for this once again does nothing but supplant the reality of the true Master with the illusion of the universal mind power. Granted, the height of the universal mind power can be achieved, but ingress into the purely spiritual regions is not possible without a Living Master's divine accompaniment. Without a Master Guide illuminating the Inner Path, the way can become perilous and the goal remains distant and dimly lit. However, with the conference of true initiation through the agency of an authentic Master, the individual's own soul self is miraculously awakened, allowing one to suddenly enter an entirely new life lived in truth, love, and a never-ending expansion of consciousness.

CHAPTER SEVEN

YOU ALONE ARE THE OBJECT OF YOUR SEARCH

Soul's divine journey is saturated in ecstatic bliss, divine wonderment, and unprecedented revelations of truth, wisdom, and the realization of our indelible connection to God the Oversoul. This journey of soul is unparalleled, incomparable, and is considered by the Saints to be the ultimate pilgrimage ever known to humankind. It is the divine heritage, the inalienable right, of everyone to tread this sacred inner Path, and irrespective of external conditions or circumstances, no one is ever excluded.

To afford yourself the glory of these divine promises requires nothing but a heart full of sincerity and a palpable yearning to discover first your own essence, and then the essence of your Source. No other requirements are needed, for the spiritual desire to return Home is always sufficient in the eyes of both the Saints and of God. It is only our own emotions and mind that have erected the barrier between soul and God, for there is no amount of romantic reverie or mental powers of reason and logic that could ever bridge the infinite abyss between soul and its Creator. To transcend the vicissitudes of mind and emotions, to banish the karmic burdens that enslave us all, and to restore the self-luminous vision of soul's innate nature are the goals and aspirations of all spiritual seekers. But to shoulder the burden alone, to rely on the strength of your own intellectual acuity and analytical mind, is similar to attempting to lift yourself by your own shoe laces. Clearly, it is a self-defeating proposition.

The Lord knows of our weaknesses, the heartaches we have endured upon the many twists and turns in the road, and of the anxiety of our high-paced living, which merely leads to our eventual demise. The Lord knows of our frustration, our loneliness, and our hidden despair, but despite all of this, the Divine Creator has lovingly promised all sentient beings that they will never be forgotten or left alone. The Lord has made provisions, for His divinely appointed Saints have been sent to light the inward Path, illuminating the eternal Way for those who are stumbling and struggling in their endless search for truth.

With the precise counsel of the Living Master and the celestial Sound which He brings, all spiritual efforts turn into visible gain, and no lesser power can ever again delay or detour the infant soul. Armed with the Master, the truth, and the Sound, the soul rises like the phoenix and is never again required to imprison itself within the human form. The crowning glory of all spiritual pursuit is for the individual to become a Saint oneself rather than worshiping at the feet of the Saints, to become the living embodiment of truth rather than searching for it in the ancient spiritual scriptures, and to realize that one's own body is literally the temple of God, not the holy shrines and architectural wonders of the world.

The following story of the wandering seeker adequately portrays soul's plight within the lower worlds, along with its incessant search for true happiness and the pearl of great price.

THE PARABLE OF THE WANDERING SEEKER

There once was a man who constantly searched for the secret to his happiness. This man knew that since no one was really happy, including himself, there must be a hidden secret to ultimate bliss and fulfillment. He knew there was a secret to wealth, love, friendship, and popularity, and so he naturally felt there must also be a secret to everlasting happiness, and he was determined to find it.

So, the man first embraced the secret of wealth and amassed great riches. He then pursued the secret of love and was blessed with a good wife and many children. And finally, he gathered a cadre of friends and became the most popular among them. But even though he was very thankful for what he possessed, there still remained a void of emptiness that called out longingly within his heart. The man eventually concluded that the secret to happiness did not lie in the temporal gains of the material world, and so he assumed that it must lie either within the pursuit of the psychic arts or the traditional religions. He dabbled in spiritualism, psychic healing, and positive-thinking mind theories, but rather than shedding the karmic barriers that held him prisoner, he seemed to have acquired more. He then became a Hindu, a Buddhist, and finally a Christian, studying diligently the Bhagavad-Gita, the Dhammapada, and the Holy Bible, gaining wisdom and knowledge from them all. But the ultimate secret to his happiness still eluded him, causing him to become visibly distraught.

Much like a wildfire, his unhappiness consumed him, for this wandering seeker had seen his entire lifetime pass before him, but he had not yet achieved his goal. Thus, while lying feebly upon his deathbed, he summoned a wise man and put a heartrending question to the noble sage: "Where did I go wrong? I pursued and attained all of the goals and ideals available in society, and I was a faithful devotee of every religious institution and psychic art known, but I openly admit that I have not discovered the ultimate secret to my own happiness. Can you offer to me, oh wise man, any wisdom on my plight?" And the wise man said,

"My dear seeker, you have wandered endlessly and externalized your search, pursuing the secret to happiness in all the wrong places. Please realize that the hidden secret is this – you, and you alone, have been the object of your search all along. The secret to lasting happiness is within you. Apply yourself there."

That very hour, the noble sage gave to the elderly man the secret of his own inner kingdom, fulfilling the answer to the wandering seeker's lifetime quest for nothing other than himself.

∼⌒

The wandering seeker's dilemma closely parallels the predicament that all humankind finds itself within, for no one is really happy within the world, even though the pursuit of happiness is a God-given quality and is only natural. Some would object to the basic premise of this statement, but the Masters would then rhetorically ask: How could anyone truly be happy when one's very own soul is imprisoned within the cage of the body consciousness, and the principles of karma and reincarnation are being levied against one? Most individuals attempt to discover the secret of true happiness by externalizing their search, but they are looking for truth in all the wrong places. Absolute truth has never been found, nor will it ever be found, outside of the individual's own consciousness.

In our search for this elusive happiness, we oftentimes mistakenly rely upon the pleasure principle, but when our pleasure turns to pain, we realize we have fallen for a temporal illusion. This futile chase can persist indefinitely, for the mind within the human being is stolidly convinced that truth, bliss, and happiness are certainly outside its own mental capacity and the parameters of its own intellectual atmosphere.

The wandering seeker was only in search of his true self, and since he was the object of his own search, the answer he sought to the secret of eternal bliss and lasting happiness could only be derived from his realization of this great truth. It is far wiser to seek the eternal soul dwelling within you than it is to chase temporary happiness through materialistic acquisition or to blindly follow the concepts and ideas of others. The entire strategy behind this wondrous creation is for each individual to discover and then ultimately realize one's own true self. No other purpose exists. Thus, the sooner any seeker recognizes this foundational truth, the sooner one's life will come into spiritual order, and all of the lower powers and forces will then rush to serve one.

The wandering seeker was informed that the secret to happiness was within him, and that he should diligently apply all of his efforts in this inward direction. Only by retracing our footsteps back to the third eye is our own inner Path revealed. This is what is meant by the statement "the MasterPath is within you." When this sacred inner Path is followed, the spiritual goals of illumination and enlightenment, liberation and emancipation, Self and God Realization, and eternal salvation are attained, and then it is you, and you alone, who wear the crown of your own Mastership. Within the folds of your own inner consciousness do the soul, the Sound, and the Lord reside, and so too does the entirety of the Lord's magnificent creation. In short, you are the way, you are the truth, and you are the life.

The soul is not foreign to the region of Sat Lok, the glorious realm of the Absolute Lord, for this was its original abode before the creation of time and space. In the soul's descent from Sat Lok within the devolutionary cycle, it acquired the numerous coverings of the lower vessels, finally emerging on this physical plane enshrouded with a mind, emotions, and a physical body. These encasements greatly dimmed the soul's effervescent and luminous nature, forcing it to repeatedly wander from the cradle to the grave remaining unaware of its innate divinity, much like a glowing lantern smothered and doused by heavy layers of thick blankets.

And so, upon the cycle of the great wheel of life and death did the soul begin to spin, and it was catapulted through countless incarnations of differing species too numerous to count, evolving through the vast spectrum of life forms within the wondrous realms of creation. When the soul finally attained the human form, it began its steady ascension from the primitive consciousness to the human consciousness, and likewise, from the human consciousness to the spiritual consciousness. The human experience incorporates all three of these levels of the evolving consciousness, which in the physical body are represented by the lower three chakras, the higher three chakras, and the third eye aperture, respectively.

The Masters of Light and Sound stress the importance of beginning the process of concentrating soul's scattered energies at this third eye aperture, as opposed to the recommendations of some of the occult and yogic practices that focus on the lower bodily chakras. The Masters also shun the forces of the kundalini and prana energies, for these are motor currents within the body and are meant only for its sustenance. The Masters teach their aspiring students how to collect their sensory currents, which are the powers and energy of soul that are externally reflected in the body consciousness as the attention. Wherever we place our attention determines our present reality, for the experience of pain, misery, happiness, or contentment can only spring to life when our attention spotlights its specific reality.

Thus, the spiritual practice within MasterPath basically consists of collecting and gathering this very quality of attention day by day and gently centering it within the third eye focus. By placing the attention in the third eye and holding it there, the diffused sensory currents within the body and the outside world begin gradually withdrawing, first back into the body, and then consolidating upward into the focus of the third eye. Many seekers of truth are not sure if they know what the third eye is or where it might be located, and they strain their physical eyes or mental senses to find it. The third eye is just above and behind the two physical eyes, so by simply closing your eyes, you can actually enter the third eye. If this explanation is still insufficient, then try shutting your two physical eyes and simply imagine your friend, your mate, or anything else familiar to you...you are now residing within the third eye aperture.

As our concentration begins to improve, both the light, in the form of knowledge, and the Sound, in the form of love and bliss, begin manifesting within the perceptual consciousness of the third eye. As our sensory currents are increasingly gathered, the veil separating the physical and astral worlds is lifted, and the doorway leading to the first level of Heaven is flung open. It is in this new world of heightened consciousness that we rendezvous with the Inner Master and receive His blessed Sound Current. The sacred journey of soul has begun at this point, for at this stage the chela realizes that soul is the true disciple, not the mind. On the wings of the Sound Current, coupled with the Inner Master's flawless guidance, the soul is now free and unencumbered to begin sailing the seas of the higher consciousness.

Therefore, one of the initial objectives of the Masters of Light and Sound is to reveal that the mind has usurped soul's spiritual throne. The mind poses as the darling of the universe, and yet we know that our very own mind is seldom happy or fulfilled. In a world filled with endless variety, the mind jumps from one pleasure to another, from one opinion to another, just hoping to find that eternal contentment that seems to elude it. The world is transitory, impermanent, and constantly changing, and for this reason the mind's attempt to stabilize itself through the pursuit of desires, passions, possessions, and personal relationships can only bring temporal appeasement.

Along with the mind's futile attempt to find lasting bliss and contentment, we must consider the inherent nature of the lower creation itself. It does take some time for all human beings to realize that our earth world is not the Shangri-La that we had hoped it to be. On the contrary, the Masters instruct that the world is a training ground, a remedial prison house meant for the liquidation of humans' accumulated karmas, and its sole purpose is to teach them the deeper lessons of life. Both the world and the mind exist within the play of the dual forces, endlessly being moved by the pendulum of life that constantly swings between the two poles of day and night, love and hate, and morality and immorality. Many times, the denizens of this world expect life to serve them, pamper them, and entertain them, and while this occasionally transpires, more times than not we are left in some type of mental, emotional, or spiritual quandary.

And so, along with our uncertain mind that must live in a constantly changing world, we must also understand that there are karmic lessons assigned to each individual dwelling in these lower worlds. You cannot exist in this physical world unless your karma has demanded your presence. Life's experiences are assigned to everyone, for the spiritual intent of the earthly life is to gradually unfold the

inner consciousness. The soul, through numerous incarnations, gradually scales the evolutionary ladder, preparing
itself to eventually embrace its own realization of self.
Thus, we are not just haphazardly thrown into these materialistic regions for no reason or purpose. Each and every
separate incarnation is meant to gain ingress into the meaning and overriding purpose of life, to discover the unrevealed
depths and talents of our own inner consciousness, ultimately allowing us to develop a greater working harmony
within our own composite nature.

Therefore, our companion mind, the external world in
which we live, and the karmic lessons required to evolve
our present status are continually at play, and they typically
create more disharmony than not. Naturally, in a scenario
such as this, the soul eventually yearns for true knowledge,
real purpose, and a deeper sense of bliss and contentment
that is permanent and unchanging. This gives rise to the
spiritual pursuit, and many lifetimes are afforded the soul
to acquire this steadily evolving consciousness. The vast
multiplicity within the spiritual pursuit, that is, all of the
various approaches, whether metaphysics, philosophy, or
religion, systematically provides experiences that further
shape, mold, and reframe the soul's idea and concept of its
very own self. In time, the Light and Sound Teachings are
revealed to the traveling soul, and preparations are immediately made to finally exit this theater of action once and
for all.

The salient point to grasp and ultimately realize is
that the gifts of God, the qualities we need to peacefully
and harmoniously live within ourselves and the world, can
only begin to manifest once our vision is turned inward
toward the eternal verities. Only at this propitious time
does the inner consciousness begin to fully perceive that
truth, God, and the indwelling soul cannot be discovered

through the conventional approaches offered to human-kind. The search for the everlasting and supreme consciousness must be conducted within the laboratory of one's own inner being, and once this is seen, the seeker need only find a true Path, a true Master, and the true Spirit, for the final escape from these lower regions is not possible otherwise.

Upon the advent of these divine Deliverers, the fledgling soul is finally ready to begin its instruction regarding the last remaining barrier to be conquered, which can be identified as one's very own individual mind in its three separate manifestations, i.e., the conscious, subconscious, and unconscious minds. The soul, now armed with the sword of truth, protected by the Master's universal love, and employing its newfound power and wisdom, step by step learns to control and rise above its own mental and emotional forces, regaining its spiritual freedom and sovereignty incrementally. The soul finally transcends its greatest foe and enemy, which in truth has always been its own lower self, not someone else or some other external condition or circumstance. Having found itself at last, the soul liquidates its remaining karmic obligations and brings spiritual order to its life, no longer deriving its sense of well-being and happiness from the world of the sensory-intellectual consciousness, but now from the lofty pinnacle of the spiritual consciousness.

With the daily performance of a spiritual exercise, the scattered and diffused sensory currents of soul begin focalizing within the third eye, and daily strides are made toward securing a lasting peace and newfound equipoise. Thus, the student must systematically transcend the confines of duality within the world at large, one must rise above those nagging karmas that constantly assail one, and one must move ever-closer to the headquarters of soul and mind within the tisra til. These pivotal efforts will unquestionably bring untold spiritual blessings, a new and revitalized meaning and purpose to one's life, and will provide a constant source of love, bliss, peace, and expanded awareness.

The spiritual method employed on the MasterPath to gather the scattered sensory currents from the body consciousness and draw them back into the third eye is called contemplation, which is natural, easy, spontaneous, and can be performed at any time. Contemplation is far superior to the method of prayer, for prayer simply invokes the divine mind within the individual and creates the illusion that one has a personal relationship with God. In truth, an individual's prayer can only elicit a response from lord Brahm, the ruler of the lower realms of the creation, and Brahm cares only for the mind, neglecting the soul entirely.

When comparing the practice of contemplation with meditation, several distinctions between the two methods clearly stand out. Meditation strives to still the mind completely, while contemplation allows for an interrelationship with the mind. Meditation requires one to employ rigid self-control with an admixture of force and pointed exertion of the personal will, while contemplation allows one to relaxedly ponder and muse over a selected spiritual subject or truth. To achieve noticeable results in meditation requires two or three hours of daily practice in total seclusion, while in contrast, contemplation can be successfully performed in twenty to thirty minutes. Not everyone is able to assume the correct posture in meditation, but in the performance of contemplation, any comfortable position will suffice. And meditation strives to invoke transcendental visions, while contemplation centers solely upon the expansion of consciousness and enlargement of one's own inner awareness. MasterPath simply stresses the importance of doing a contemplative spiritual exercise for approximately thirty minutes each day.

The MasterPath embodies the pursuit of true spirituality and cannot be confused with any type of psychic, occult, or religious endeavor, nor can it be perceived as a means of escaping one's present responsibilities. The moral and ethical standards for a student of Light and Sound are no less than traditional religious expectations, and in fact, they are far greater. The initial aim of the seeker is to master the karmic principle, not to become even more deeply enmeshed than before, and so our character traits and the quality of our behavior gradually refine themselves as our level of consciousness expands.

As the consciousness rises upward, the student finally realizes that it is not the world that needs saving, but only oneself. Aspiring students also come to understand that they must save themselves, rather than merely depending upon an ascended or a Living Master to do it for them. The Path back to the Godhead has room only for one, and so the individual must oneself become the pilgrim on the Path. The Master and Sound are situated close by, constantly guiding and protecting, but spiritual evolvement is for the individual alone, and so full culpability must be taken in one's spiritual ascent.

The MasterPath teaches that all austerities, whether rites, ceremonies, the quoting of religious scripture, attendance at religious gatherings, public prayer, or acting as an emissary for one's chosen faith, have no actual bearing upon your spiritual ascent. All of these aforementioned practices and observances adorn only the mind, and little if any spiritual uplift can be derived from them. This is not to imply that these austerities have no practical value, for the individual and universal minds are nurtured and directed through these performances. However, according to the Saints and Masters, any spiritual observance that does not arouse or resurrect the soul has little spiritual import or appreciative value.

For a student of MasterPath, the majority of one's energy will not be applied to invoke God's attention, mercy, or good grace, but to adjust to the power flows and gifts one is already receiving. Time should not be wasted in calling out to God, but should be given to actually living the life of God. The religious or metaphysical mind is unable to do this, for only the soul can pattern itself after God. The mind is restricted to merely imitating or parroting God's divinity, but the soul was created in God's divine image, and so the clarion call to be as perfect as one's Creator in Heaven can only be successfully achieved through the innate divinity of soul.

The mental and intellectual senses of humankind were never intended to replace the spiritual senses of soul, and in truth, they are not capable of doing so. The three-tiered complex of the mind was initially created to assist the soul in the lower three regions, i.e., the physical, astral, and causal/mental planes, but the intent was never for the mind to take on the responsibilities reserved only for the soul. Humankind's spiritual heartaches, its spiritual barriers, and its spiritual bankruptcy are simply due to the mind's attempts to act in the capacity of the soul.

The mind has not been properly equipped to live the spiritual life, but if the soul is not presently awake, the mind is forced to fill in. In the soul's absence, the personality is given birth, which has a litany of attending powers to support it. The personality mistakenly believes itself to be the real and true self, and it has a difficult time grasping and understanding what the Master means when He states that one must realize the true self, for the personality assumes it already knows who it is. The personality, through the lens of the mind, actually does know itself, but it does not know, nor can it ever perceive, the divine self. The personality is referred to as the false self, while the soul is termed the real self. Thus, to replace the false with the real, and to then wed absolute truth in place of relative truth, are the spiritual objectives to be achieved, the former being Self Realization, and the latter God Realization.

In closing, I would like to offer a brief summary of soul's divine journey, including both its initial descent and its ultimate ascension back to its regal realm of origin.

SOUL'S DIVINE JOURNEY

From the very beginning, ever since the soul first descended from Sat Lok, it had been desperately in search of itself. In the course of its sojourn, soul innocently identified first with the materialistic world, then with the personality of mind, and finally with lord Brahm, but all were eventually exposed as mere paltry reflections and shadowy representations of the true and eternal self.

In its long and unimaginable saga, soul embodied the human form time and time again, playing the roles of father, mother, daughter, and son literally thousands of times, but in the end, soul clearly perceived that it was actually none of these.

The soul gave its allegiance to country, state, and the color of race, and so too did it identify with countless creeds, spiritual methods, and moral and ethical precepts. But in the dawning of its realization, soul easily perceived that these were only temporal and partial substitutes.

The soul endlessly roamed the physical, astral, and mental realms, ceaselessly experiencing the cycles of birth and death, but with its restored and clarified vision, it realized that none of these regions were in reality its true Home.

Soul shouldered the weight of lifetimes of karma, forced to initiate involuntary causes and to then live out their ensuing effects, while it was helplessly spun on the wheel of karma and reincarnation. But since then, soul has replaced the law of karma with the law of grace.

In the sunset of its journey, while assessing its great wealth and surveying the reasons for its success, the soul cannot help but ponder the benevolent Master and the majestic river of Light and Sound, for only through the assistance of these incomparable gifts from Lord Anami did the forlorn soul find its way Home.

Finally having merged with God's true Essence, soul regally reclaims its throne and is flooded with bliss and ecstatic joy, for it too is now crowned and counted as one of the heavenly Saints.

～～⌒

If it takes a lifetime to find a true Master, the arduous search has not been in vain, for one's cup must be emptied in order to understand its fulfillment. Everything becomes known through the concepts of contrast and comparison, and so the secret to true and lasting happiness can only be recognized and attained through the long march of unfulfilled promises and crooked avenues that abruptly lead to countless dead ends. Thus, to all of you wandering seekers, wander no more, for the Camino Real leading directly to soul and your Creator is indelibly etched within you, just awaiting your recognition.

CHAPTER EIGHT

THE MASTER RESPONDS TO SEEKER INQUIRIES

1. **Q.** Sri Gary, things that seem to satisfy others do not fill my emptiness, but I keep chasing them anyway. Is there a purpose behind all of the futility and disappointment in life?

A. That is a wonderful question, and I am happy to offer you my heartfelt response. Before turning to Spirit, truth seekers are going to follow every desire, urge, and pleasure they possibly can. They may buy the perfect home, get the new car, and amass abundant possessions; they may find Mrs. or Mr. Right, explore love, get married, and have many children, but eventually they will come to a screeching halt. When does this screeching halt manifest? When they are at total odds with their own lives.

Individuals who have had a difficult life and are very weary from chasing life's pleasures are actually quite fortunate, because they have begun to realize that life is not as pretty, perfect, and romantic as they were told it would be by their parents and society. Thus, when they have had enough of the endless futility of trying to find happiness by changing their immediate circumstances and external conditions, ironically, they find themselves in the deepest level of bondage they have ever experienced. This is when the true seeker will turn one's face toward the spiritual pursuit.

So, if you are experiencing this sense of bondage within your present life, please do not be dismayed. This is one of the Divine Deity's supreme intentions – to entice the soul to begin questioning what is transpiring within one's life. One of the primary objectives of the mundane, physical life is to allow the individual to finally see that life's conditions are so empty and dreary, so boring and mundane, that one just finally has to ask, "What is going on? This just does not make sense. There must be some level of truth, a deep, hidden meaning that I am missing." And indeed, this assessment is true and correct.

There are countless enticements in life that are intended to entrap us. How about the passions of the mind, such as anger, lust, greed, vanity, and attachment? How about bondage to our children? What about bondage to our mate? If someone's companion translates, oftentimes the partner left behind does not have enough strength to stand on his or her own. This is bondage. How about bondage to drugs, money, or to desires not yet realized? What about bondage to anger, and desiring revenge against certain people who have hurt us? Prior to realization, our bondage is prevalent and operational in almost everything that we do, say, or think.

But dear one, here is the true message regarding all of these seemingly futile and disappointing experiences: When you have really experienced the depths of this bondage, you develop a sense for freedom never before known. You want freedom so badly it becomes palpable – you can taste it. When you desire freedom from the very bondage you have experienced, that is the beginning of spirituality. True spirituality is not for those who just want to make their outer lives better, whether through a new mate, job, car, or a bigger paycheck. Actually, these very desires are what you want freedom from, for they are not delivering the fulfillment and happiness you seek.

There is an axiom, a self-evident truth, used by all Saints, even though many do not agree with it. This axiom states that no one is truly happy in this world, meaning that if the true self has not been found, one cannot be truly happy and dwell in the spiritual states of consciousness continuously. Now obviously, not everyone in our world feels they are unhappy, and in fact, it is quite the contrary. With all the pleasures and play toys humans can buy to keep themselves outwardly occupied, there is hardly any time for them to look at their own inner condition, for they are totally preoccupied and attached to outer stimuli.

But for a spiritual seeker, even if things are going quite well on the outside, there is still a gnawing, unsettled, subjective reality present that is squeezing one: "I am not as happy as I want to be. Yes, I have enough money, a loving family and children, and I am very thankful for that, yet, I feel unfulfilled." This is Spirit knocking at your door. It is your higher self saying, "There is more, you do not have to live this way." As a seeker, you can certainly be relatively happy in many ways and yet remain unfulfilled in your heart of hearts, and this is what matters. Whether you are at the end of your rope or not, if your heart is in some way breaking or yearning for more, then you know you are not completely happy in this world. I was certainly knocked around and was brought to my knees until I could simply say, "I want Spirit more than I want my desires or my favorite pleasures." If this was true for me, then I know the same is true for others as well.

So please do not regret what you have experienced in the past, for thank God you did. Thank God you have been shaken up by the karmic life force. There are certain causes you have put into motion, and the effects of these causes have brought you to your knees. Thank God. When you really want the higher meaning of life, you can have it, and this is what the MasterPath is all about.

I want you to know that I am not allowed to persuade you in any way, nor am I looking for more students. All I want to do is to help those who want to help themselves, to assist those who are seeking their own spirituality and are trying to get in touch with their own true selves. True spirituality deals with making your spiritual self superior to all lesser realities, such as the mind, emotions, impressions, social conditioning, desires, and all of your karmic obligations. True spirituality transcends everything temporal and empirical, allowing you to ascend into the beauty and height of truth, consciousness, harmony, bliss, and love. These are the spiritual realities that MasterPath aspires toward and spiritually embodies.

2. **Q**. I am interested in this Path, but whenever I try to write a letter to you, the fear of what I might have to give up stops me. I don't want any more pain or sacrifice in my life. Are these fears warranted?

A. Absolutely not. Spiritual unfoldment deftly eliminates pain, it certainly does not create it. Please understand, however, it is the subconscious that experiences an aversion to pain. It primarily wants food, shelter, and love, and it simultaneously strives to avoid all pain. So the fear here is real, but as you said, it is a fear of perceived loss, not growth. The subconscious mind does not want to strive for something it feels it already possesses. You see, the mind is so bloated and full of itself that it feels it already contains all there is. This means that the mind is willing to laterally develop, but it is not willing to vertically develop because that may mean death to its own ego and personality. This death of the ego and personality is what the crucifixion symbolically represents. In fact, this is what the story of the crucifixion was meant to convey, not the death of Jesus.

The soul within each of us is the true Christ, and the crucifixion is just the sacrifice of the lower self, or the mind/ego.
Our true identity is soul first and foremost, and the ego and
personality of the mind comprise the false self, which has
pulled a power play on the soul. The mind has only borrowed its glory, power, energy, and indeed everything else
from the soul, and then it postures itself as the originator
of them.

So, the fear that can arise when you consider the
spiritual pursuit is merely the subconscious mind reactively
saying, "I do not want to sacrifice any part of my life. I
love my pleasures and all my good times, and I have things
the way I want them. Why should I disturb this?" This is
really a very interesting conundrum, because once someone does taste the higher consciousness, they find it hard to
understand why they waited so long to take the next step.
And yet, on the other hand, we can be extremely fearful
and even angry about having to sacrifice anything in the
initial stages, and so this is no laughing matter at all. I won't
tell you not to worry about it, because I know the fear is
real, but if you can understand that it is only your subconscious refusing to let go of what your mind mistakenly
thinks is divine, then you can transcend this subconscious
fear and continue on with your spiritual pursuit.

The mind never really feels that life can be better than
what it is right now, and this is the greatest illusion our fear
and anger weave. The soul within knows better. This is
why we are all striving – because we know, from a much
deeper level, that there must be more than what our fear
and anger are representing, protecting, and expressing.

3. **Q.** I have been searching for over thirty years, and I
have studied many paths and doctrines. I get very involved
at first, but then my interest wanes. Why is this?

A. Thank you, for you have asked a very universal question. First, may I say that if you have found a path or doctrine that you resonate with and have happily embraced, do not leave it, but stay right with it and take it to the very end. The Divine allows us to be attracted to nearly everything that exists within life, including all paths, doctrines, and truths. We live so many different incarnations that eventually we experience everything in life, naturally evolving the quality of our search. The Divine has instilled a type of self-destruction system in everything within the lower worlds. Whenever you imbibe in or partake of something, whether marriage, children, collecting cars, or being a bum, you are initially attracted by it and find reason to be there, but eventually you find it no longer fulfills you and you simply lose interest. This same principle can be seen with children and their toys, it occurs to all of us with lovers and mates, it manifests in our occupation, and it most certainly transpires in our search for truth.

Seekers, true seekers, are those who yearn for God and truth, and they never rest until they discover the level of truth that is relative to their own present experience. If Buddhism is someone's truth for this lifetime, that individual will not rest until he or she is a good Buddhist. If metaphysics is the destined karmic pursuit for someone who currently happens to be a Christian, that person will carry religion only so far, and then suddenly it will fizzle out, and he or she will feel a strong magnetic attraction for some type of metaphysical study. The point is that first there is an initial attraction, and then in time, there is an aversion. This is inherent and purposeful, and it can be defined as the intrinsic nature of all experience in the lower worlds.

We are all destined to arrive back to our spiritual Home, fully realized in soul and having found ourselves in

God. This is why billions and trillions of souls are here in the first place. And with this as the divine objective, you can easily see that whenever you are involved in a mere relative part of the absolute whole, as purposeful as it may be at the time, you will eventually grow weary of it, and will naturally be drawn to something else even more pertinent and spiritually valuable to you. Whether this takes one day, fifty years, or an entire lifetime is entirely up to the individual.

4. **Q.** I know several people who are atheists. Is there actually a spiritual purpose in not having any spiritual beliefs?

A. There is great purpose, for all of the varying degrees of spirituality exist because of the myriad levels of soul's ascending maturity in Spirit. We have souls in the world who are not ready for any form of outer spirituality, and they need to just experience the world on its own terms. This is as much spirituality, although in a lesser degree, as someone who is actively walking a path to discover God or to understand more about the Divine. I can unhesitatingly tell you that the highest path for anyone is simply the path which that individual feels he or she should pursue. If that means no path for some people in this lifetime, then they should not be on a path, but should just live out their lives in the best way they see fit. All individuals have their own calling, which must be respected. No one should be judged or demeaned because of what one does or does not choose. This is not as much a moral issue as it is a deep spiritual insight. Every possible experience is part and parcel of God's universal body, and through necessity, each one has pertinent value to the soul's evolvement.

5. **Q**. I have read that this level of spirituality requires a readiness in the heart. Does that mean that certain people are not qualified for a Light and Sound Path?

A. Well, it is certainly true that an endeavor like Master-Path is not for the masses; it is for readied souls. However, anyone can enter this Path, whether one is a man, woman, old, young, Hindu, Buddhist, Christian, or of any particular race, for none of these external distinctions make a bit of difference. The Path is not exclusive in that sense of the word; it is inclusive. There is a point of wisdom that must be grasped though, for in order to move onto the twelfth grade, an individual must have finished the eleventh. Someone who is in the eighth grade cannot just jump to the twelfth grade, because there would be no way for this individual to digest the instruction at that level. This is where the Light and Sound Teachings become exclusive. The only individuals who will be attracted to a Light and Sound Path are those who are at the end of the road with their present experience, whether it is a religious, philosophical, or metaphysical endeavor. After the soul has experienced countless incarnations attempting to find God, one's spiritual desire naturally evolves into what you could call "a readiness in the heart."

When someone is truly ready to embark on soul's divine journey, that individual will experience an undeniable attraction when coming into contact with these Teachings, and this is the only qualification needed. There is a wise saying from the past that states: When the student is ready, the Master will appear.

Souls come into this world and pursue spirituality for many, many lifetimes, and when they reach a certain point in their spiritual evolution they are literally "called" by the Divine, the highest spiritual Power situated within their own inner being. It is not the Master who calls, and it is not your own pleading that brings you to the Sound or the Sat Guru. Thus, it is not your decision, nor is it mine. Souls who are ready to connect with the Teachings of Light and Sound simply feel an undeniable magnetism and draw in their hearts, and this is the call of the Divine. Even if you experience some type of contention with the Living Master initially, either how I look, talk, or carry myself, that is still inconsequential, because if you are ready, the divine Power within your very own soul will move mysteriously and touch your heart in ways you have never before experienced. It is the Divine who calls, and when the Divine beckons a soul, no one has the power to waylay or ignore Its call. The principle of spiritual attraction is behind this "being called," and so whatever is needed in order to experience greater growth and unfoldment in soul will automatically be placed before you.

6. **Q**. I love the writings of some of the great Masters like Kabir, Hafiz, and Rumi. I am also attracted to you as a contemporary teacher, but I feel inadequate about my ability to walk this ancient and sacred Path. Sri Gary, my life up to now has been anything but spiritual, but I still feel a great draw toward these Teachings. Could I possibly be a candidate?

A. What you are really saying in asking this heartfelt question is, "I have read about the Teachings and I feel drawn and inspired, but am I ready...me, in my ignorance, my poor grades in school, and the numerous times I have failed in life...am I ready for a Path like this?" Well, I say there is a good chance you are, for you would not feel such magnetism or attraction if you were not deeply and properly prepared.

There is a very important principle that you should be aware of as you are assessing your readiness for the journey of soul. Universal law states that every move you make to better yourself must be challenged by a counterforce. This applies even to something as trite as trying to do the dishes. A counterforce will actually come up and try to stop you from simply cleaning up your kitchen. There is always a counterforce in life, and the same is true in spirituality. The ego and mind want to remain in control, and so they will instigate an enormous controversy to keep the discovery of soul at a standstill. I just want you to be aware of the fact that if you are going to make a move toward your own emancipation, you will run into barriers that will require you to prove your sincerity, to prove that you want truth, love, and Spirit more than you want your life of untruth. This is the most honest I can be with you about your own mind's diabolical attempts to disqualify you from the Path of truth. The present concept you have of yourself has been created by your shadow, your lower, negative self. I would love for you to have the opportunity to experience your own soul, for then you can redefine yourself in divine love, spiritual power, and true freedom.

When the Sound, which is pure consciousness and pure love, becomes dynamic and active within you, the soul awakens and all life changes automatically. Your awareness will amplify exponentially, and the solutions to all of your questions will appear before you in a moment's notice. This is why there is so much love, joy, and conviction emanating from those who do follow the Light and Sound Teachings, for they are pointedly experiencing the fruition of their own consciousness, and God and consciousness are woven from the same identical fabric. So, to answer your question of whether you may be a candidate for a Path such as this, I want to tell you, yes, your magnetism suggests that you are, but in truth, you must make this decision for yourself.

7. **Q.** There has to be a purpose in life greater than the events in my daily life. What is the reason for our existence according to the Light and Sound doctrine?

A. Any true Master of Light and Sound will tell you that there are only two primary objectives in the world: first, coming to know your true self, and second, coming to know God. We have a human body in order to discover our own spiritual essence, and for no other reason. We are not down here simply to create a family, we do not incarnate just to work on an assembly line, and we are not here merely to find the ideal mate or to wear beautiful clothes. We are here to eventually realize that we are exactly like God. In soul, we are a drop of pure Spirit that is identical to the Divine Ocean, and this discovery is termed Self Realization. The entire purpose of life is to discover, to realize, that you, in your true identity, are soul. This is life's divine purpose. As the ancient directive says: Man, first know thyself. When you find out who you really are, this is referred to as Self Realization, and it is at this critical juncture in life when you are then able to truly come to know Spirit and God.

So, there is one main priority in life, and that is to first discover and then pursue who and what you truly are. This spiritual attainment is all that interests a true Master, or Sat Guru. A Master's entire mission is to help lead readied souls through the spiritual journey. He assists and guides His students through their own limited body/mind identifications, inspiring them to further concentrate and center their attention energies in the third eye. At this point, they are finally able to leave the body consciousness (or body identification) and ascend into the consciousness of Self Realization, and eventually God Realization.

At best, the Living Master is a guide, a counselor who points the way and offers instruction and direction. What a Sat Guru knows, and you have yet to realize, is that you are the eventual Master. A Master's mission is to direct His students to their own Mastership so they can experience life through their own God enlightenment. The Master wants to help, He wants to guide, but the entire accent is on the individual coming into one's own Mastership. This Path is called the MasterPath because it is the Path to your own Mastership. There is no possible means by which the soul within you can transcend the lower worlds and get back to Heaven until you ultimately realize your own Mastership within yourself. As Jesus and other Light and Sound Masters have taught: Ye too are the Sons of God.

8. **Q.** Sri Gary, I have read some of your spiritual writings, and you are very clear about the difference between conventional religion and true spirituality. But you have referenced Jesus Christ as being a great Saint and Master several times. I am not sure if you uphold Christianity or not. Will you please offer clarification?

A. My good friend, there is a vast difference between what Jesus Christ literally stated and what the religious historians have attributed to Him. There is equal disparity between what Jesus Christ actually meant and what has been interpreted through the minds of religious authorities spanning the past two thousand years. And so the answer to your question is both yes and no. If you are asking whether I believe in institutionalized Christianity, my answer is "no," but if you are referring to Christ's original Teachings, my answer is "yes."

Jesus Christ's original Teachings were pure, and as a genuine Master of Light and Sound, He expounded on the Light and Sound principles throughout His mission. However, He never wrote a single word of the Bible, nor were any of His Teachings even recorded until decades later. With the expansion of the clergy in the early church under Roman rule and their efforts to dehumanize Jesus, along with Constantine's sanction of Christianity as the religion of the empire and his open support of the Council of Nicea, and with the many alterations, omissions, edits, and numerous translations of the Bible, it is rather surprising that it has survived as well as it has. But to uphold its complete authenticity and reliability, as though everything written fell straight from the lips of Lord Jesus, is both illogical and romantically naive. It is far better, in the eyes of the Masters, to place your trust and faith in a living embodiment of God, as opposed to a holy book or an ascended Master. It is important to state, however, that in the absence of a true Master, thank God the holy scriptures and ascended Masters are available to help those who need them.

9. **Q.** I understand your writings to say that there are passages in the Bible that reflect or are similar to what you talk about. I never heard any religious authority from the church speak about karma, multiple Masters, or the third eye. Are there any examples you could offer from the Bible that corroborate the Light and Sound doctrine?

A. Your understanding is absolutely correct. The Holy Bible itself is a spiritual cache of immutable truths, and many passages are in complete agreement with the Light and Sound principles. Thus, the immediate barrier seems only to be the angle of vision that one employs to interpret these scriptures. In viewing through the lens of the mind, the individual either extracts a literal or a figurative interpretation, an exoteric or an esoteric understanding, pointing to the great principle that you can never be greater than the concept you hold of yourself. In general, truth seekers first perceive and then follow either the letter or the Spirit of the law, and this choice determines how any devotee will ultimately interpret one's own holy scripture.

There are many biblical references that clearly substantiate the same principles that the Masters of Light and Sound represent and uphold. For example, the Masters point out that the higher levels of Heaven are within you, and similarly, the Bible states, "The Kingdom of Heaven is within you," and "In my Father's House are many mansions." The Masters emphasize that the soul reposes itself in the third eye and that all worship commences from this sacred temple. Likewise, the Bible states, "Know ye not that ye are the temple of God, and that the Spirit of God dwelleth in you?" The Masters of the Light and Sound unanimously declare that one's scattered sensory currents must be consolidated back into the third eye to receive illumination. Likewise, in the Bible it is stated, "The light of the body is the eye. If therefore thine eye be single, thy whole body shall be full of light," and also, "God is a Spirit and they that worship Him must worship in Spirit and in truth." The Masters of Light and Sound lucidly explain the inexorable law of karma, and biblically this principle is stated as, "Be not deceived. God is not mocked, for whatsoever a man soweth, that shall he also reap," and similarly, "For every man shall bear his own burden."

There is also biblical scripture which confirms the spiritual mantle being passed from John the Baptist to Jesus, and then from Jesus to Peter, verifying the Light and Sound principle that there is an ongoing line of Masters, and that there is always at least one true Master present in the world. Jesus confirmed this same principle in part when He said, "As long as I am in the world, I am the light of the world," clearly suggesting that His divine mission lasted only as long as His earthly incarnation. Regarding the principle of reincarnation, Jesus made it lucidly clear while talking to His disciples that Elijah had returned, and was now known as John the Baptist. Any logically thinking individual can surmise what this literal statement means.

It should be noted, however, that this corroborating biblical evidence is not sufficient for emotionally thinking devotees, as they are unable to subject their own chosen beliefs to a higher mental scrutiny within themselves. There is just too much fear and uncertainty that surround their own thought processes. This is one reason why the Masters state that only the bold and daring can find the absolute truth, for it runs counter to the comfort zone of the conditioned "mass believers."

The text of the Bible is comprised of mere paper and ink, while the Word, or the Sound Current, is the Power that actually created all things. A close study of John 1:1 reveals this great truth, for it qualifies the differentiation between the Holy Bible and God's Holy Word, or Sound Current. Interestingly enough, this very point lies at the core of the inevitable fate of all religions, because when their founding Saint departs, shortly thereafter the relevant scriptures are unwittingly used as a substitute for the live Presence of the absent Saint. The beauty and eloquence of these holy scriptures is unquestionable, and the wisdom within the parables so universal and enlightening, but the scriptures still remain a sterile and empty shell when directly compared to the illuminating and life-giving forces of the actual Presence of the founding Saint.

When there is a Living Master at the helm, the arguments and dissension that naturally arise over theological hairsplitting and differing interpretations of the scriptures come to an abrupt end, for the Living Master serves as a present embodiment of the true scripture. True scripture is not reading about your Master, but living in His eternal Presence. Why labor over the meaning of words and scriptural verses when you can actually physically hear and listen to the true Master? The clergy simply lack the knowledge of the transcendental, the esoteric, and thus are innocently unable to articulate, let alone interpret, the majority of the spiritual mysteries. You cannot expect to receive enlightened commentary from unenlightened beings. This is really no fault of their own, for most religious authorities were incompletely schooled, as were their teachers. As Matthew 15:14 states, "Let them alone. They are blind leaders of the blind. And if the blind lead the blind, both will fall into a ditch." This is why a Living Master is so essential, if for no other reason than to correctly interpret the riddle of the scriptures and the spiritual mysteries.

10. **Q.** I recently read one of your books, and even though I very much want to raise my spiritual consciousness, the thought of leaving my religious beliefs and the church behind is quite frightening to me. Can you offer me any guidance?

A. Thank you so much for having the courage to ask this question, and please know that there are many others who also struggle with this same issue. First off, let me say that you do not have to relinquish your chosen faith to raise your spiritual consciousness in degree. Those who are happy with their present teaching should stay with it and just strive to be better devotees, whether they are

Christians, Hindus, or Buddhists. They should simply follow assiduously the spiritual recommendations of the founding Saint of their chosen doctrine, whoever it may be. To illustrate, the Christian should strive to be ever so still in one's prayer, collecting one's attention and focusing it in the single eye in anticipation of the visitation of Christ in His Glorified Body, and to then receive His instructions on how to proceed further upward. Yes, it is true that according to the Light and Sound doctrine, exclusive contemplation on the Two Faces of the Master, both the Outer and Inner Forms, most greatly facilitates and expedites the upward movement of consciousness. But if you are still deriving benefit from your present religious association, then you should not strive to replace your current, chosen belief.

Since you mentioned your fear of leaving the church, I assume you are perhaps a Christian. If so, please also consider the fact that the term "Christ" was not part of Jesus' proper name, but was a title, an anointing or conference of a higher level of consciousness. There are numerous Christian devotees who strive more for the Christ consciousness, or the "Christ-like mind," rather than the externalized devotion and worship of the man, Jesus. Nevertheless, in either case, reliance is still being placed exclusively upon an ascended Master, and this greatly reduces any chances of a lasting success. In religious terminology, success entails eventually becoming the Christ oneself, fully realizing that one is already a son or daughter of God, thus viewing oneself on equal footing with the great Jesus the Christ. Attainment of the Christ consciousness is actually akin to cosmic consciousness, or realization of the divine mind, although it still falls short of Self Realization, which transpires within a region situated one plane further up.

As far as the guidance I would offer you, at this time I would actually recommend that you stay with your present belief until you have exhausted all benefit from it. You will know, in the depths of your heart, when you are ready to take another step.

11. **Q**. Sri Gary, would you please offer clarification on what you mean when you say that truth is instilled within the soul before birth?

A. Certainly, I am happy to expound on this subject. The only way of returning back to God is through our own soul, which is located within our own body. True spirituality was bestowed upon us in the form of the soul long before we ever came out of the highest regions of Heaven. The true religion, or the ability to commune directly with the Spirit, was given to the soul long before a physical world even existed, long before there were books, and long before any external religions were created. Humans created the outer religions, but God created the soul, and the true religion lies in each and every soul.

This truth is what the Master Saints wish to teach, reveal, and ignite within the sincere seeker's heart. Yet, most seekers run to every corner of the globe trying to find what is already present within them. A true Master will simply redirect you to look for the pearls and jewels of spirituality within yourself, not in any book, not in another individual, not in a denomination, and certainly not in some remote foreign country across the seas. Every human being houses the perfect Path within his or her own body. Thus, the Master simply guides and directs His students to retrace their steps back to their own inner temple within their own precious bodies, for it is there where they will meet their own true selves.

Every human has this innate religion within oneself, even before one's physical birth. This is the way that God remains in contact with humankind, and it is also the way humankind can make contact with God. It is the perfect religion, and no human being can alter it. No one can add one word, for it is final, complete, and perfect. It is fascinating to ponder over just how the Divine Deity could create a Path that everyone would be able to find when the time was right...and of course, all that the Supreme Deity had to do was instill this Path within the very essence of the soul itself. Therefore, the true Path resides within your own body, and you need only go within to find it. Jesus Himself taught: The road is narrow and few be there that find it.

In contrast, religions, philosophies, metaphysical sciences, and psychosomatic practices have all been created by human beings. For instance, what Jesus told His disciples in a closed room versus what He told the masses was completely different. As I stated previously, Jesus did not create Christianity, but it was the disciples who turned Christ's Teachings into a religion following His death. Humans have created all religions and all philosophies. Strong-willed people, accompanied by strong opinions, have done so from the very beginning of time. All existing religions will eventually fade out, and in their place other religions will come. They too will fade out, and still others will come. All existing religions have had a beginning, and all religions will have an end, for this is the fate of anything created by humankind.

As it stands right now, the West is in the throes of seeing religions crumble. It is witnessing multiple paths, their leaders, and the priestcraft's limitations being exposed. We are in a state of turmoil, and yet, ironically, more than ever before, humankind needs spirituality. So what is the problem? Why is all of this happening, and why are so few really having success? Why are the churches crumbling? Why do we see so much deceit? Why is the younger generation so dissatisfied with what they have been told is spirituality? Well, the simple reason is that most have not yet found the original truth you inquired about. It is there, and you can find it, for it is actually closer to you than your own heartbeat.

12. **Q**. I understand that the soul is within me, but why do I not feel connected to my soul or higher self? How has this happened?

A. In order to begin to understand your current condition, first you should be aware that both the soul and mind are knotted together right between your two physical eyes. However, because you are currently unable to stabilize your attention within this spiritual center, soul's energies have escaped this chakra and have dropped down into your body, animating all of the glands and lower chakras therein. So, the vast majority of your energy is scattered throughout the bodily chakras and is now highly influenced by your emotions and mind, as well as your karma, possessions, likes and dislikes, and even your loves. Of course, you desire to be spiritual and have a calling inside to draw closer to Spirit, but yet, this is impossible when your energies are still down in the bodily chakras and are not centered and consolidated within the third eye.

Most seekers have heard of the chakras within the human body, but I will offer a brief review. First is the elimination chakra, and its function is not merely elimination, for in spirituality this chakra represents your will power. When your energy initially drops down into the body, it manifests as the personal will. A degree of personal will is necessary in life, but usually we see far too much of it being expressed. Through the personal will, the mind takes the spiritual energy of the soul and utilizes it to perpetuate its own ego-based, personal agenda. In contradistinction, when one's energy is centered and held within the third eye, the individual displays a much more spiritualized universal will.

The next chakra, the reproductive chakra, is enormously powerful. Consider just the power of the sexual energy alone. The magnetism and drawing power of the reproductive chakra are overwhelming to most people, and thus large amounts of spiritual energy escape through this aperture.

As we ascend up the spinal ladder, the next chakra is the navel. This center controls nourishment, not only in relation to food, but in a larger sense, to anything that we use and rely upon to nourish our lives. Far too often, we use the objects and possessions to which we are most attached to nourish us – for instance, the love we develop for our house, our car, or our new little computer. Many times we use things to nourish us that are not spiritual at all, and the result is the loss of considerable spiritual energy through the navel chakra. On the other hand, when our energy, or attention, is centered and held within the third eye, we are continually nourished by Spirit through Its divine grace and love.

Next is the heart chakra. Here a majority of energy is lost because this is the chakra where love, relationships, companionship, and our social consciousness are created and birthed. Can we agree that most people feel lonely and somewhat isolated, and they are looking for someone they can love who will make them feel good, who will make them feel whole? This is why we have an innate and inherent desire to find a mate, a love, someone to merge with, both physically and emotionally. This desire comes from the heart chakra. We expend a lot of energy hoping that what we really need is "out there" and chasing after the perfect family or the ideal relationship. Certainly, relationships and family can be marvelous experiences, and I am a very happily married man myself. However, for too many it becomes the ideal – the ultimate ideal. Much of our personal love is largely emotional attachment and is very, very conditional. Conversely, when our energies are centered within soul's vibration at the third eye, our love becomes unconditional and universalized. A much deeper and fuller love than emotional love manifests...a love that truly passeth all understanding.

The throat chakra is the last major bodily chakra that needs mention at this point. Simply put, the throat chakra expresses the play of your mental senses. All logic and reason are reflected from this center, as it is the first thinking center void of all emotional influences coming from the heart. Rather than feeling as though you are an emotional being, at the throat chakra you will relate to yourself as an intellectual being, and this is the physical ego's first expression of itself through thought. Yet, your true identity in soul is still situated above within the third eye.

Before you can truly commune with the Divine through pure consciousness, you must first come to know your own self. You must come to know your own essence, and in order to find your essence, your true spirit, or the soul self, you must ascend your energies to the third eye. The soul is presently asleep, and so its energies have been usurped by the physical and mental senses within the human consciousness. In all simplicity, this is the dilemma, this is how our connection to the soul and Spirit within us is temporarily severed. Our own ego and the endless desires of the body and mind are the culprits.

13. **Q**. I am very concerned about losing my individuality in a spiritual pursuit. Is that a valid concern on the Master-Path?

A. No, certainly not. The Master's entire purpose is to restore your individuality, and the Supreme Deity's main consideration is the preservation of your own individuality as well. How could anyone stand in the Kingdom of Heaven any way other than by being an individual? This is realization of the true self – the ability to identify and express your own life force, unencumbered by the mind and ego. This is true individuality. In all its simplicity, the MasterPath involves the process of discovering who you are. Your true identity is the soul, the divine spark that exists within each one of us. This spark within you, which you presently know nothing about, is pure, eternal, immortal, and full of bliss. It has access to all information, comprehends all knowledge, contains all wisdom, and is comprised of pure love itself. Soul has the power to live life in total harmony with both the Divine's plan and the individual plan simultaneously.

Thus, the road to the Divine, to your own Self Realization, is your way – your own individual way. You do not conform to mass rules, nor do you ascend in or through the collective consciousness of the masses. If there are two thousand people in a room, there are two thousand different ways for each of them to return to the Godhead. While you go through the process of realization, you must "be you" in order to penetrate your own karmas, to fully experience and vitalize your own unique, personal journey. Only by individually being yourself can you first discover, enliven, and then completely express this divine spark of God, which is who you really are in truth and in Spirit.

14. **Q.** I have difficulty giving my trust because I feel that other spiritual teachers have exploited me, and I'm very wary about opening up again. Can you shed some light on this dilemma?

A. Absolutely. To me, your question is extremely important because many spiritual seekers experience this very burdensome, almost overpowering dilemma. They are simply seeking the truth, but nearly every time they reach out in an attempt to discover truth, they are shortchanged, taken advantage of, and exploited, perhaps by some cultish group or a strong personality. Far too often these types of paths and gurus have ulterior motives. They are usually not interested in the seeker's beingness or realization, and more times than not, even if the pseudo gurus are sincere, their own realization is generally incomplete. Therefore, their teachings, their doctrine, and their methods have many limitations and can only reveal relative levels of truth. So, not only is it difficult to find truth, but once you do decide to search for it, many roads are necessarily traveled, and many levels of relative truth must first be experienced.

The journey of soul is orchestrated in such a way that eventually seekers will naturally exhaust the relative level of truth they are currently experiencing. They come to realize that the path they are embracing does not completely fulfill them, and in a moment of clearer perception they realize it is not the end, but only a means to the end. Sincere seekers who are actually ready for the absolute truth of Self Realization usually experience this.

The true Master is fully aware of this process, and His students are the ones who come to see this. The Master knows that each seeker will be pulled along, even through many difficult experiences and heartbreaking letdowns. He knows that all souls are hungering for truth, and that each one will eventually be drawn to His door. The Master is very aware of this type of external dilemma and the exploitation which often accompanies it. Thus, He also knows that one of the resultant effects is that seekers of truth generally do not trust anyone.

Another aspect of the seeker's dilemma is the fact that one does not even trust oneself. One day you feel you know it all, and the next day you know nothing. This is the internal dilemma, or simply stated, the problem of one's own mind. So yes, spiritual seekers are doubtful, and they should be. They have been externally exploited by others, and internally exploited by their own minds. Many are so disillusioned by these repeated experiences that they just close themselves off and crawl into a protective shell. It is all very understandable, but please never give up hope...the Divine loves each of Its children so much that this Power has actually placed a part of Itself within you. The heartbreak and betrayal you have gone through are simply part of a greater spiritual process and a much larger picture than you are presently able to perceive.

Now, in contrast, those individuals who have made a decision to investigate this Path have experienced, each in their own way, the sublime reality of Light and Sound, for these individuals have gone a little bit deeper. They have penetrated some of these issues in degree, and so they have been willing to allow the Master to prove Himself to them over time. This type of provisional faith allows one to taste and directly experience the Sound as It comes through one's own beingness, and this is the only surefire means of progressively removing all doubts and skepticism.

15. **Q.** Will you please address how and why the mind creates such havoc within us?

A. The mind has the power to disrupt your viewpoint in the moment, but the power or vibration that has been divinely created to energize, empower, and control your own body, your entire life, is your soul, your true essence. However, due to the power the mind possesses, which has developed over an enormous span of time throughout the many lifetimes we have lived, the mind has over-powered the soul and usurped its position. Mind has led the way, mind has done the thinking, and mind has done the contemplating. Basically, the mind and intellect have created and produced all of your opinions, conclusions, conceptions, and perceptions. And, may I repeat, we have all been around for a very long time. Thus, the mind and its reasoning faculty, along with the evidence of the physical senses, have outcreated the soul – your very own precious soul. This means that when soul wants to give you a message or inspire you with divine love, a higher truth, or greater spiritual wisdom, ninety-five times out of a hundred it will be outcreated and overridden by the evidence or arguments of your own physical and mental senses.

In fact, this is also one of the greatest obstacles the Master must deal with, for His own students, as well as many well-intended seekers, usually view the Master and the Teachings in the same way they have experienced everything else throughout their entire lives – through the construct or vehicle of the mind. The mind is a machine, and it cannot even truly exist on its own, for the mind derives all of its power from the soul within the body. The mind alone cannot love, it cannot think, it cannot induce or deduce, nor can it initiate any action through its own volition. In all cases, one's energy is first generated by the soul and it then filters down into the mind, allowing the mind to act in its mechanical and conditional ways.

Many seekers assume they know what true spirituality is, but truth be told, ninety-five percent of their thinking has actually been given to them prepackaged. Nearly all of the images, thought forms, and knowledge that we possess prior to realization have been borrowed from someone or something, for there has been very little experience on our part to create real, firsthand knowledge.

Therefore, in this ignorance, we relate to the highly conditioned and largely preprogrammed mind as our real self, or our true identity. We adopt the mind's perspective, and we rely on it to guide us through life and to regulate all of our actions. Worse yet, we invoke and engage the mind to perceive, self-evaluate, and judge ourselves. But eventually, we catch the ego one day claiming, "I am really quite evolved and there is no one greater," while the next day it is found complaining, "I am no greater than a swine, and I do not even know how to tie my own shoe laces." The spiritual seeker must eventually understand that the mind vacillates up and down like this constantly, and if you are honest with yourself, you will definitely be able to perceive this ceaseless vacillation in your own mental atmosphere. With time and effort, the mind will become a very good servant to soul...but in the absence of soul, it is a very poor master.

16. **Q.** I do not mean this disrespectfully, Sir, but at times I feel I have an obstacle in relating to the concept of a Living Master, and yet, I am still interested in investigating this Path. Is there an explanation for this?

A. This is an issue that affects many sincere seekers, so first, please allow me to restate and lovingly reaffirm that the soul is a drop from the Divine Being, and thus it has the same attributes, the same omnipresence, omniscience, and omnipotence as the Divine. We are truly Gods...once realized. Nothing can touch the soul – not poverty, not pain, nor the pleasures derived from the fulfillment of desires. Soul is so strong and powerful that it can literally be as big as the universe. But nevertheless, difficulty can arise, my fellow soul, when the spiritual seeker attempts to evaluate a Master. The nemesis here is that even though soul is the true identity, hardly anyone is perceiving through the eye of soul.

You are currently viewing all life through your mind and mental senses, and therefore your perception of the Master, the Path, and what the Master is saying is in direct proportion to the present level of purity within your own mind and mental senses. For this reason, much of what the Master wishes to convey to you is not going to go as deep as He would love for it to, and in fact, chances are you are going to throw up a wall and keep Him out completely. This is the number one obstacle the Master faces, and of course, the seeker as well.

The Master understands and is acutely aware that sincere seekers desire truth very much. All they want is love, honesty, and true spirituality, but the mind stands in between their desire for truth and the message of the Master. As a result, some seekers only receive little tastes or fleeting glimpses here and there, and even this is only when the cynical, critical mind relaxes a little bit. But when the mind actually does allow the power of soul into one's perception without prejudging, then one's point of view enlarges and the simplest statement can take on a new and more profound meaning. Yet, the mind is usually so self-centered and self-absorbed that it often feels it already knows all things, and so it passes judgment freely and without reservation. The mind can take a purely heavenly situation and turn it into hell, manifesting an unbearable nightmare of pain, anguish, and confusion in an instant.

Regardless of this, I actually welcome you to study and observe me through your mental senses, but please just be aware of the inherent nature of your mind, for the message of Sound, Spirit, and the Sat Guru is intended to address the soul within you. Spiritual truth circumvents the mind entirely, even though many times the mind will try to understand what is being said, almost as though it is a life or death issue. The mind, through intellect, reason, and logic, futilely attempts to give truth some type of meaning and form, but in reality, truth does not even exist within the levels of the mind.

Truth is a vibration that resides above all duality, above cause and effect, and far above the mind. The attributes of the mind (intellect, reason, logic, and discrimination) are all by-products of the universal mind power, and yet these are the tools we initially use in our spiritual search. We must recognize that our very own mind is composed of positive and negative vibrations, and that all life contains these dual properties as well. Before I can discuss what truth is, I have to discuss what it is not. As you observe life, you will find that everything has this stamp of duality: male/female, good/bad, love/hate, day/night, truth/untruth, awareness/lack of awareness, knowing who you are/not knowing who you are, etc. Duality stamps everything, and the mind can only operate through this construct of the dual forces.

The mind is a great pretender. We can walk about in the outside world in nice clothes, we can drive new cars, we can live in beautiful homes, and we can project ourselves to our friends and neighbors as someone who has "got it together." This is just the mind projecting its pride and vanity to others. When we are alone in the privacy of our own room, however, we do not feel quite the same way. This is an example of the mind's inherent duality. There are always two sides to any issue when viewed through the mind, but truth always remains singular.

So, your hesitancy to embrace the Master is actually a natural response emerging from the dual nature of your mind. If you can suspend your wariness long enough to allow yourself the opportunity to gain some firsthand experience, you can yourself put these fears to rest.

17. **Q**. You have spoken and written about karma, but will you please offer more about what karma is and how it works? How does it relate to the concept of destiny, or fate?

A. Your question certainly addresses one of humankind's great dilemmas. First let me say that if you had no karma, you would be in total bliss right now. You would be full of love, and you would instantly leave the body/mind consciousness and rise up to the higher states of awareness and joy – instantly. It is karma that keeps us chained to the earth, and whether it is levied against us as iron shackles (difficulties) or golden chains (pleasures) makes no difference. All souls must eventually clear their karmic account if they want to ultimately achieve the higher realizations. Your problems in life, your heartaches, the loneliness you experience, the people that judge and demean you, the dissension and arguments you have with your boss or loved ones, your difficulties with your children, how you think, how you look, when you were born, when you translate, and basically everything else that you do in your life...all is regulated by the law of karma.

In simple terms, karma is the law of cause and effect, meaning whatever action an individual puts into motion is a cause, and according to spiritual law, there must also be a corresponding effect. As Jesus taught, "As ye sow, so shall ye reap." If we initiate a loving cause, a loving effect manifests. And likewise, if we put forth a negative cause, a negative effect will follow. This is the principle of karma. Please understand that whatever you think or feel about people and conditions in life are actual causes, and this takes into account and includes all of your deeds as well. The Divine has structured our world in such a way that we will eventually experience the direct effects of all of our own creations, or causes, and this is the purpose of the karmic law.

Humanity is either unaware of or very lax regarding the karmic principle, and thus continually generates causes that create karma, or indebtedness. This karma then accrues to levels that are completely impossible to negotiate and spiritualize in a single lifetime, and reincarnation is therefore set into motion so we can return to the physical world to gather the fruit of both our good and bad karmas. Please understand that karma is always remedial and not punitive. This is the divine law, the real justice and universal fairness that permeates all life. The karmic principle exists simply to allow soul to gradually awaken and unfold beyond the selfishness and limitation of the human condition.

Through the creation of both good and bad karma, souls are inexorably bound to the great wheel of birth and death, upon which they are forced to spin for literally millions of years. This cyclical repetition of birth, death, and rebirth has been metaphorically referred to as the "wheel of eighty-four." As long as karmic debt remains on the physical plane, the individual must return to fulfill it. This nearly endless up and down motion within the lower planes is the basis for the metaphor of the wheel of eighty-four, or what is commonly known as reincarnation. The only way to get off this wheel, the continuous cycle of birth and death within the physical, astral, causal, and mental realms, is to attain Self Realization, which is the first major goal of the MasterPath. When you can transcend the play of this big wheel of karma and reincarnation, you can then put an end to the ongoing cycles of birth, death, and rebirth. This is not to imply that there is an end to our life, or consciousness, for the consciousness of soul is the one unchanging reality that just continues to expand into the regions of pure spirituality, far beyond duality and the law of cause and effect.

All of the circumstances and situations in your life are therefore due to your own karma. They are your earned and created fate, or destiny. Simply put, everything in the lower worlds is karma. Thus, our destiny, or fate, has certain experiences in store for us, and we will inevitably be drawn to these experiences. Certain people will cross our path that we are destined to meet, the mate we are supposed to marry will be drawn to us without fail, and any children we may have will typically be souls with whom we have shared karma in past lives. In truth, everything is so perfect and tightly knitted together that to question, discount, or deny any aspect of your own life, whatever is presently in it and why you are experiencing what you are, is really a misunderstanding of divine law. Everything that has come to you has done so with great purpose, divine meaning, and spiritual intent. Karma is not meant to punish, but to teach you a life lesson or to give you a spiritual insight in order to reveal a greater truth. All life is so perfect that it would really behoove everyone if they could accept their own unique and individual position, regardless what it may be. If you feel miserable, then first of all, accept that you do. Do not deny or self-medicate to escape the problem, but simply accept it. A miserable feeling should inform us that something is amiss, that there is something we need to change or outcreate through a higher viewpoint or a higher state of awareness. However, if we do not accept the fact that it is perfect for us to feel this way in the moment, then we can never rise above the nagging condition, objectively examine it, and see the lesson or greater opportunity being presented.

So, karma is most definitely related to fate, or destiny, in the conventional way we understand these terms. The Master's sole objective is to reveal to you who you are. The Master wants you to become your own Master, and likewise, the Lord wants you to awaken in soul through Self and God Realization. This is the overall objective of life, and so this is our true destiny. Therefore, all life is going to serve this process, and this defines karma's relationship to destiny. Whether we realize it or not, it is our karma that continually propels us toward the ultimate goals of the spiritual life.

18. **Q**. I have always struggled with the theory that those who have great success in life are blessed by God in some way, and those who don't are being punished by God. Is there any truth in this concept that some people are inherently good while others are inherently bad, or evil?

A. Oh, what a marvelous question, for it reaches into the heart of truth. First off, the Divine Creator loves each and every soul equally. What you are really asking about involves the principle of karma. There are many ways to approach the topic of good and bad karma, but I would like to begin by briefly reviewing the origin of the terms "good" and "bad." You will not find one thing that is whole in and of itself beneath the soul plane. All life and all conditions within the lower planes (physical, astral, causal/mental) exist in relation to their opposites. This is because of the division that occurs when the formless One, the Sound, descends and is diluted into form and light. This is where we encounter the concepts of sin and righteousness, good and bad, love and hate, and all of the apparent dualities of life.

In truth, our own relative viewpoint is what actually creates all such dualities. The mind is and always has been the culprit which divides the oneness of truth, or Sound, and picks and chooses, or creates individual distinctions of good and bad. And nowhere is this determination of what is essentially good or evil more important than when it comes to the orchestration of our present lifetime's circumstances, which, of course, are dictated by the conditions stored within our karmic account. Prior to incarnating in any given lifetime, humans have the opportunity to choose how certain positive and negative karmas will be utilized within their upcoming incarnation. This selection is not made from the pristine, elevated viewpoint of the soul, however, for it cannot be unless the soul is realized. So the choices made are from the relative viewpoint of the entity's current unfoldment up to that time, from the position in consciousness to which one has evolved.

Therefore, since many souls are still maturing and are not yet duly prepared and ready for the experience of Sound and the Sat Guru, they will often utilize whatever positive karma they have accrued to create a relatively easy, or positive, lifetime condition for themselves. They often incarnate into more technologically advanced countries and societies or perhaps into affluent families within lesser developed societies. Such individuals usually, though not always, become more educated than others and experience a relatively high standard of living when compared to the global norm. Of course, there are also many souls of a more evolved nature who choose to utilize their positive karma in a higher way, which is to incarnate into circumstances and conditions that will test them spiritually. They choose life conditions that will provide more of an opportunity to confront their own limitations and to grow and evolve in a spiritual sense.

The true value of these lower worlds is that they allow us to have a multiplicity of experiences, even though many times they are not very pleasant. We are constantly battered and beaten in life, and many things can just go sour on us, for our fondest pleasures often turn into our archenemies, and our greatest loves can become the source of our deepest sorrow. Herein lie the ultimate value and purposeful nature of our karma. Simply put, karma provides the preparation, growth, and unfoldment through the light and duality that are needed before the soul is ready and willing to experience the Sound.

The Divine loves each soul so much, and the Lord actually yearns for all Its children to return to their true Home, which can only be experienced when the individual soul is realized and thus liberated. Therefore, the Creator has ensured that there is always a true Master present in the world, and at times, there is more than one. The true Master's only mission is to gather souls who are ready to exit the lower planes, the dual worlds of experience – that is His only mission. So, those souls who have chosen to use all of their previously accrued good karma to acquire a meeting with the Master instead of the new home, the lovely children, or whatever the desire body may consider happiness to be, are truly blessed. If you find that many of the "good" things in life have been denied you, rather than assuming you are not in God's favor, perhaps there is a greater purpose. As a seeker of truth, there is a very good chance that you have wisely chosen to use your good karma to earn a meeting with the Living Master. The true Master will not let you down, betray you, or forsake you in any way. If you are strong in your desire for truth, the Master will in time prove to you, beyond any doubt, that through this very choice, you have come to understand and completely transcend the value and purposeful nature of karma.

19. **Q**. Despite my best efforts to live the spiritual life, the stress of dealing with the daily challenges I face seems to diminish or even cancel out any gains I make. What I would like to know is whether this is self-created or is it due to conditions and circumstances outside myself?

A. Personal responsibility is the key attitude we must develop in order to transcend or outcreate our karma. What a beautiful system the Divine has created for us all, and yet, we can still sometimes harp on others or place the blame with them for our own current state of consciousness: "He did this or that to me," or "The boss does not understand who I am," or perhaps, "My lover does not understand me," or "Why am I going through all this grief?" The beauty of life, of the divine law, is that no one can hurt you but yourself. Nothing is happening to you except the effects of what you have created, either in this life or a past life. You create a cause in thought or deed, and there is an equal and opposite effect. That is how the system works – cause and effect. No one is punishing you, nor are they responsible for your current attitudes and feelings, your state of consciousness – only you are. When you are able to take charge of your own causes, or actions, this will naturally spiritualize all effects that come to you as a result of those actions. Only then can your karmic burdens begin to dissolve.

Taking charge of and being accountable for your own actions, or causes, is spiritual responsibility. This is the beginning of true action and true spiritual living. We are responsible for everything we have in our life, good or bad. All of our conditions in life are meant to help us come into greater harmony with divine truth and principle, to serve us, to teach us. This is the attitude we must develop and perceive from when viewing all circumstances and conditions in our lives. Without this armor of personal responsibility, we live in a state of reaction and continue to sow the seeds of karma, reaping only further karmic effects.

Many people have developed a strong sense of personal responsibility, and their unique journey of soul has brought them to a position where they recognize, at least in degree, that they are responsible for much of what exists in their lives. Only a rare few have evolved to the point of accepting complete responsibility for everything. Those in the former group are partially successful in transcending or outcreating aspects of their karma, but how are we to rise above this level of partial success and limited results? You can only transcend your karma fully when the soul is realized. Only when you elevate your attention and energy beyond the lower planes and live life from the elevated perspective of the realized soul, fully attuned to the Sound Current, can you completely outcreate karmic tendencies, for these tendencies thoroughly penetrate and rule the physical body, as well as our emotional and mental selves. I wish to be very clear that only through spiritual unfoldment, or awakening the soul to the point of genuine Self Realization, can our karmic attitudes, beliefs, and modes of behavior be fully transcended.

Truly taking charge of your own behavior and becoming fully responsible for your causes are the results of awakening the soul. Living beyond the reach of karma is one of the great promises of the Path of Sound, and of course, it is also one of the primary objectives of the student. Once you are established within the soul consciousness, there is little chance that karma can touch you, simply because you have risen in consciousness above the dual forces of life, the polarities of good and bad, or right and wrong. When the soul is awakened to the point of Self Realization, you now have a vehicle, or faculty, that is in resonance and harmony with the Sound Current. You can tune right into the essence of any given situation, event, or subjective thought or feeling and manifest truth, Spirit, and love in the moment. You are no longer the effect of karma, social conditioning, tendencies, and the past. This is the true freedom of Spirit that all sincere seekers long for – and you can have it.

All of the precious souls in the world have experienced and are experiencing problems and situations in life relating to their karma, whether it be a drinking problem, a drug problem, a relationship or work issue, melancholy, boredom, or even depression. The true Master wants only to help the soul, and this is the Inner Master's area of expertise. The Inner Master literally yearns to work with sincere chelas twenty-four hours a day, for it is His duty to assist them in unraveling the burdens of their karma, whether it consists of iron shackles or golden chains. A genuine Master can and will assist you in consciously coming into contact with your own soul, your own true and divine essence, and then together, from a position in consciousness that is above the mind and all duality, you and the Master can ferret out the causes behind all of the crippling effects you are living under and then straighten them out. Some can be rectified almost immediately, while others may take the course of a lifetime, if you are sincere. May I say, karma is actually a puffball – it is literally nothing, for it lacks real substance. Once we are able to transcend the mind, then all karmic tendencies, demeaning behaviors, and questionable attitudes are exposed for what they are – simple limitations in viewpoint, not solid, immovable realities.

20. **Q**. Sri Gary, I have a rather strong aversion to becoming part of a group or spiritual movement, but I do want the assistance of a true Master. I don't think I am a typical spiritual seeker, and so I am wondering if you would work with me individually to resolve my own unique issues or if the MasterPath would require group involvement and effort?

A. Oh, yes, absolutely, the individual relationship between the Master and the student is central to the process of unfoldment. Let me begin by first saying that the MasterPath has nothing to do with the group consciousness – all unfoldment is an individual affair. The moment a seeker becomes a chela, the Inner Master begins teaching you as an individual and preparation begins for the second initiation, which is when the Inner Master permanently stations Himself within your third eye chakra. Every one of us is sacred, every one of us is a child of the Divine, and every one of us is going to walk the Path back Home in a little different way than our friend or neighbor. We have all come from a different place, not in terms of where we were created, but regarding the experiences we have had in the thousands and thousands of lifetimes in our past. We are all at a little different place in consciousness, and in fact, no two souls can occupy the same space at the same time. We all exist and live in varying states and levels of consciousness, and thus the Master works with each individual on one's own level. Our unique individuality is a gift that just keeps taking on greater and greater form as we develop and move closer toward the Godhead.

So, the Master does not care where you came from or what type of unique karmic burdens you are carrying. They are insignificant to the Master. Would a father and mother be concerned that their infant child could not talk yet, or had slurred a word, or wet his or her diapers? Of course not. Nor is the Master concerned with your present baggage or your level of unfoldment prior to even beginning the Path of Sound. It will take time to unfold and develop a level of spirituality within you that will allow you to clearly see and understand those things that are currently driving you half mad, and the Inner Master will assist you every step of the way.

The Inner Master is all things to all people, and so when He comes into your life through initiation and stations Himself in your third eye, you, yourself, are the king, not only for the day or the week, but for your entire lifetime. You are the one the Path centers around, and so if you perceive some current limitation that is not up to par according to your point of view, please do not be too concerned. These karmas will not be addressed until you get further along in your spiritual journey. We all have something hidden in our closet, and regardless what it is, the Master will work with it and help us. But we must be patient and realize there is no way we can let a limitation go unless we find something better with which to replace it. No individual can be expected to live a pure and moral life if one has not yet awakened to soul and experienced the joyous upliftment of the Sound Current. The Master will love you even more than you hate your own defilements, attachments, and desires. The true Master will work with whatever karmic tendencies you have, whether they are weak, strong, mildly disturbing, or even very pressing.

These karmic conditions are primarily dealt with at night in the dream state, for the Inner Master can work with you much more effectively when your conscious mind is at rest or sleeping. But day by day and month by month, you will become increasingly aware of this inner work, and your daytime hours will be filled with new revelations, insights, and inspiration regarding whatever karmic situation is manifesting in your life. New attitudes will begin to emerge, affording you fresh and much more encompassing viewpoints that will easily ameliorate or completely dissolve these old nagging problems and limitations that have plagued you.

The Outer Master's role in the chela's karmic condition is merely to instruct one on the spiritual principles, as well as how they should be applied to one's attitudes and viewpoints in order to live life more harmoniously. But as a chela, you can experience truth much more directly than this. If you have a question, you can go inside to the Inner Master and present your question to Him. For example, you might say, "I have a major problem with this element of karma. I have been trying to reconcile this, but I have not been successful. Will you help me?" The Inner Master will say, "Of course, what took you so long to ask for assistance? I would be glad to help you." The Master may do a number of things. He may bring you to the causal plane to see where the root cause, the original form of this karmic condition, began. He may supply you with the energy and inspiration needed to try once more to deal with the problem, and now, with newly acquired spiritual power and renewed energy, you will be completely successful. Or the Master may begin a process of nightly work with you on the inner planes, gradually unwinding the pent-up energy entrapped within your specific karmic condition.

When you become an initiate of a true Master, your karma is no longer strictly your own, for the Master now oversees your entire karmic account. Upon the second initiation, the Master assumes the spiritual responsibility of regulating, organizing, and distributing your karma. The Master can now orchestrate the events dictated by your karma in a progressive manner, affording you a chance to learn from your karma rather than being victimized by it. This is a huge benefit and true boon for the chela, and in fact, this is not all the Master does on your behalf. He also takes on and actually absorbs a tremendous amount of your negative karma, which allows you to focus your attention on the spiritual journey in a purer, more concentrated way. Of course, many have difficulty believing that this could possibly be true, but when your attention is able to rise to the causal plane where the karmic accounts are stored, you can see for yourself what the presence of a true Master really means in your life.

When you begin to develop consciousness and your attention and energy rise through the chakras, all of your bodies elevate in awareness and undergo a purification. Your mind becomes sharper, you gain greater control over your emotions and reactions to life, and many times your physical problems or health issues are improved. But may I add this: The Master does not simply vanquish all of your karma, for what purpose would that serve? Karma is the grist for the mill of life, and so it is by addressing our karma that we learn how to live in higher awareness. Certain karmic conditions must remain in your life to either provide necessary lessons or to pay off your karmic debt, but the Master will help you with these issues. He will help you see them in proper perspective, and He will help you cultivate a healthy, positive, and truly spiritual attitude toward your own difficulties and challenges, as well as those of others. He will be there to personally and individually assist you in the tiniest issue, as well as the most seemingly insurmountable obstacle.

21. **Q**. In your writings, you often mention the terms "light guru" and "Sat Guru." Exactly what is the difference between them?

A. First, allow me to state that there is a ladder of evolving experience in the divine system, and therefore teachers of every kind are necessary at each level. Even in the animal kingdom, there is always some dominant figure that leads the herd, and similarly, there are always more complex and evolved plants, like the Sequoias. Likewise, there are always human beings who are more complex and evolved than others, and this is why you will never hear a Saint demean another path or teacher. The Masters are required to describe the differences that exist, they are responsible for drawing distinctions between relative truth and absolute truth, and yet they will always say, "Please understand it is a perfect system and nothing needs fixing."

So there are teachers at all levels, and all of them are to be respected. They all have their place simply because souls are experiencing life at all of the multifaceted levels within the Lord's creation. The majority of human beings have their hands full with just living in this materialistic world, making a living, and dealing with their passions and day-to-day events. Then comes the long and often arduous evolution through the light, and many teachers are encountered along the way to help the soul unfold through these preparatory levels. When the student's readiness is mature, it is then, and only then, that one is truly prepared to hear and resonate with the message of the true Master, or Sat Guru.

The following two points are the simple distinctions that separate a Sat Guru from a light guru: First, a Sat Guru is appointed or commissioned to serve by the highest Lord, and second, He is fully able and qualified to initiate souls into the Sound Current. Many teachers can help you relatively, for everything has value. However, Sat Gurus are divinely appointed by the highest Lord, while light gurus are self-appointed or commissioned by lesser deities situated in the lower worlds. A Sat Guru, a true Guru, also has the spiritual power to initiate soul into the Sound, and when this happens, the entire course of the soul's journey changes from normal, mechanical evolution into spiritual evolution.

The seeker should therefore be keenly concerned about the qualifications of one's chosen guru. Both the level of initiation and the doctrine a prospective master previously embraced to achieve his or her own claims of mastership must be of the highest, for as the spiritual adage goes, you can never be more than the guru who initiated you. An individual can only attain a level equal to the heights achieved by one's chosen guru, and so if one's guru cannot reach into the higher dimensions of spirituality, then he or she certainly cannot teach the student how to do so, let alone deliver one into that higher level of consciousness. Therefore, in order for any seeker to actually receive the true initiation into the Sound Current, it must be given from an authentic and realized Sat Guru. A light guru simply cannot initiate at this high level.

Spiritual lineage is extremely important in this context, for the seeker must gain an insight into both the path and prospective master one is investigating. A true Living Master will emphatically state that anyone claiming to be a genuine Master of Light and Sound, without previously having received the true initiation from a Master schooled in the art of Light and Sound doctrine, is no true Master at all. In a world where there are more gurus than there are students, seekers must be very careful with whom they align themselves and place their trust when considering spiritual initiation. Thus, spiritual lineage serves as the seeker's major yardstick in verifying and judging a master's credentials and spiritual authority to truly initiate the soul into the cosmic mysteries. The only exception is when a Param Saint, or Swateh Saint, has been sent by Anami, the highest

Lord God, to begin a new line of Living Masters. But even in a case such as this, the Param Saint will still seek out initiation from a Light and Sound teacher and complete the basic course of instruction.

In the terminology of Light and Sound doctrine, a Sat Guru is one who can escort the soul of the disciple into the fifth spiritual region, known as the soul plane, whereas a light guru can only assist in evolving the mind through the lower planes of duality. A Sat Guru is given the divine authority to initiate the soul, while a light guru is restricted to initiations within the three divisions of the mind, which are the conscious, subconscious, and unconscious minds. These three minds are situated within every human being and distinctly operate within the confines of duality, moralism, and the karmic web of illusion and maya (delusion). A true and bona fide Sat Guru can arouse the latent Sound Current lying dormant within the seeker, whereas a light guru can only manipulate the various intellectual and psychic centers of light, which correspond to the lower dimensions within the physical or psychic bodies. A Sat Guru has the power to deliver the soul into Self and God Realization, while a light guru is more concerned with the relative levels of enlightenment and cosmic consciousness, both of which exist within the parameters of the intellectual senses.

A Sat Guru reveals and awakens the higher consciousness and restores the spiritual identity of each disciple; He escorts the soul from the tomb of the body consciousness and protects and nurtures it along the way, ultimately delivering the soul back to its original Homeland. The Sat Guru deftly shoulders the karmas of His students and protects them from the numerous pitfalls and endless snares attempting to detour them. He is a constant friend and an engaging companion, remaining with the traveling soul in all matters, spiritual and otherwise. Not even death can separate the

bond of love that is developed between the true Master
and the yearning soul. A Sat Guru has previously experienced the divine journey of soul and has fulfilled all of
the spiritual requirements necessary to attain the Kingdom
of Heaven. Thus, His wisdom is unfailing, for all of His
divine assistance and spiritual counsel are imbued with
the love and supreme guidance of the Lord. A Sat Guru
embodies and manifests the divine spiritual Current,
and He can enliven this same celestial Current within you
as well.

While light gurus do not possess these extraordinary
spiritual capabilities, they do have an irreplaceable purpose.
Every distinct level of a light guru, whether physical, astral,
or mental, has its relative purpose in the overall evolvement
of both mind and soul. Every soul, in the course of the
almost endless journey back to God, will enlist the help of
many light gurus as it evolves through numerous incarnations and multiple levels of consciousness. Therefore, a
condescending attitude or an overly critical view cannot be
taken of the multiple gradations of light gurus. Anyone
who truly understands the workings of the divine cosmology will unanimously agree that every guru and teacher
ever known in the history of the human race has had some
unique value, some relative purpose to impart to the evolving soul.

22. **Q**. I understand from your writings that you are a
Param Saint, and that even this level of Master will still
seek initiation before assuming the position of Mastership.
What was your beginning preparation and who initiated
you into the Light and Sound?

A. You are exactly right. Although receiving the spiritual mantle through credible lineage is the accepted way in

ninety-nine percent of the cases, it is not the only way. Founding Saints who descend from the heights of Anami Lok do not technically require the outer initiation, for they descended directly from the Godhead and are already divinely ignited and appointed through Anami's perfect love and mercy. This was the case with both Guru Nanak and with Swami Ji of Agra, for they were also responsible for founding new lineages of Living Masters. However, even the Param Saints must refamiliarize themselves with the Light and Sound doctrine when they enter a new incarnation. Thus, since the earmark of a Param Saint's arrival is the customary absence of a fully realized Master, in their great humility these founding Saints take initiation from a lesser order of Master, or in some cases even a Self-realized soul, and they serve and fulfill all of the requirements of true chelaship.

Although my childhood was filled with inner experiences, I was first exposed to Light and Sound on the outer in 1964 when Charan Singh Ji from Radha Soami, Beas conducted His worldwide tour and held meetings in Minneapolis, Minnesota. Following this outer exposure, I took initiation from Sri Darwin Gross in 1973, and I stayed with Him for fourteen years. Outwardly, my own experiences of devotion and discipleship escorted me through nearly all of the Light and Sound doctrines that dotted the globe at that time, including Radha Soami Satsang Beas, Radha Soami Satsang Agra, Eckankar, and Ruhani Satsang. But in truth, none of these wonderful Teachings can be given the exclusive credit for my own initiation, liberation, and ensuing salvation, for Anami Purush is my true Lord and Master. Nor is the MasterPath an extension of any of these aforementioned Paths, for it was Anami Purush who graciously sanctioned, commissioned, and orchestrated the inception of MasterPath and its current Living Master in July of 1987.

MasterPath's humble origin and the Source from which it speaks are solely an extension and direct manifestation of Anami's universal will. According to the Divine Anami's directive, MasterPath was not to become a new Teaching, but rather a pure representation of the same one truth which all Saints and Masters, past or present, have upheld and propagated throughout the march of time. Its divine objective was to be threefold: to present the true Teaching, to extol the true Spirit, and to introduce the true Master into the Western culture. A Param Saint has the sole responsibility of simultaneously reframing and presenting anew the age-old doctrine of Light and Sound, better enabling the current-day seeker to imbibe in these ancient and ineffable spiritual Teachings.

23. **Q**. I am an avid reader of differing spiritual philosophies, especially those teachings that center around the Light and Sound. I have read your spiritual writings, and they are quite lucid and clear, but it seems to me that they rather accurately reflect or are an extension of the Sant Mat tradition from the East. Is this true?

A. You are absolutely correct. As a whole, the Light and Sound Teachings have been represented by a number of different organizations and institutions around the globe, some reflecting the original message more purely than others, but all of them honoring the supremacy of these Teachings. MasterPath doctrine most closely parallels the Sant Mat tradition, or the Teachings of the Saints as promulgated by the Eastern adepts, such as Seth Dayal Singh of Agra, Sawan Singh Ji, and Charan Singh Ji. These illustrious Masters have championed the guardianship of the true Teachings better than anyone I know of in contemporary times. The major differences between MasterPath and Sant Mat are the recommended vows and the specific performance of the spiritual exercise, but other than these noted distinctions, they are essentially the same.

True Masters deftly safeguard the purity of the original Teachings, guarding against alterations, subtractions, additions, or the diluting of the doctrine into religious or psychic overtones. This gradual dilution of a doctrine's original purity has been the fate of all religions, for after the founding Saint departs and His line of chosen successors ends, the Teaching remains as nothing more than a dead mystic school, with the disciples supervising all activity and spiritual guidance rather than a true Living Master.

No one has a monopoly on the true Teachings emanating from the Supreme Deity. Therefore, the highest Lord will send a new founding Saint whenever the Teachings have lost the true Master and the principles of Light and Sound have been unduly compromised or when this Power wishes to sanction their pure resurgence in a new area or culture. Under the leadership of the founding Saint, also known as a Param Saint, or Swateh Saint, the pristine purity and spiritual luster of the true Teachings are thus re-established, and a new lineage of Living Masters is started once again.

24. **Q.** How does becoming a student of a Light and Sound Master affect or change a person's everyday life? I have heard stories in the past about certain gurus who demand large sums of money, or some who request ten percent or more of your yearly income. I have also heard of some of these same gurus requiring their students to leave their homes, their material possessions, and even to relocate and live in their ashrams. Does any of this apply to the MasterPath?

A. Thank you for asking this question, for many sincere individuals wonder about these same issues. First and foremost, every seeker must differentiate between a light guru, or a pseudo guru, and a genuine Light and Sound Master, for the two are diametrically opposed. The former is a guru of the mind, while the latter is a true Guru of the soul. A light guru encourages open battle with the mind, employing austerities and all forms of denial and renunciation. Light gurus often ask their students to forfeit their cherished possessions and to leave their homes, and they usually charge exorbitant amounts of money for their instruction. The strategy behind this seems to be the denial of the mind, in the hopes that spirituality will then somehow miraculously appear or instantaneously manifest. The illusion and failure of this approach is that wherever you go, you end up taking the mind with you, for no one can simply walk away from one's own mind. Secondly, you cannot purchase your way into the heavenly states of consciousness, no matter how much you financially give or mentally sacrifice. This would be similar to whipping the donkey because your car won't start, and nothing lasting or permanent can ever come from this type of mental paradigm.

The Masters of the Light and Sound discourage any of the above mental disciplines, and in their place recommend a spiritual methodology that centers around the soul, for the soul is the true disciple, not the mind. The Masters insist that you stay with your home, your family, your occupational interests, and all social and economic obligations. They do not ask you to renounce anything external, only to begin detaching yourself from any inner dependence you may have upon these external realities. It is this inner detachment, not the outer renunciation, which is all-important.

Moving to an ashram or a retreat is also a meaningless effort to the true Masters, for one's sacred temple of worship is situated between one's own two eyes, not in some foreign country or remote area of the wilderness.

Donating or forfeiting large sums of money in the hopes that this will somehow augment your pursuit of spirituality, or mitigate any karmic obligations, is equally misleading. In this regard, MasterPath requests only thirty dollars monthly as the chelaship fee. MasterPath is a nonprofit organization, and so it uses these funds not only to provide the study materials that are sent monthly to each chela, but also to help defray the costs of employing staff, holding public events, publishing books, and producing audio and video recordings, as well as the numerous other issues involved in making the Teachings available to the students in the physical world. In short, the horror stories you have previously heard regarding the many indiscriminate paths and gurus who exploit their students have nothing whatsoever to do with the true and genuine Masters of the Light and Sound.

25. **Q**. Sri Gary, what disciplines do you impose upon your students? I have heard in other Light and Sound Paths, mainly in the East, that vegetarianism is a requirement, and that complete abstinence from liquor, recreational drugs, and sex are mandatory vows. Two or three hours of meditation are also required if success is to be expected. How do you view these issues?

A. Excellent question, as this is what makes Master-Path so unique. But please understand that the Eastern Masters instituted these vows, and they have been very effective for the Eastern cultures. However, the supreme risk in assiduously following the guidelines of imposed vows is that one can inadvertently substitute "the keeping of one's vows" for the art of true spirituality. One can become easily swayed and pridefully arrogant in the achievement of following such vows and codes of moral conduct, but even when strictly abiding by these vows, the resultant attainments still remain within the orbit of the mind and offer no true spiritual uplift on their own. Vows are simply mental disciplines, which are imposed to help bridle the runaway mind. The MasterPath imposes no such vows upon its students; rather, the emphasis is placed on a workable moderation in all things, for nothing is unclean in and of itself.

It is only our attitude of excessive indulgence that makes anything limited or retrogressive, and so as a contemporary Master of Light and Sound, I teach my students that anything which promotes their ascension to the third eye is progressive, while anything hindering this ascension is retrogressive, or counterproductive. If you attempt to deny your mind any of its pleasures, it will either rebel or simply replace the last desire with another. The secret is to offer the mind a greater pleasure, not to take one away, which is accomplished by introducing the mind to the ever-present Sound Current. As the mind begins to enjoy the spiritual impulses and newfound meaning and energy of the indwelling Sound Current, it willingly begins to forfeit, in degree, those conditions and circumstances to which it was previously attached.

Therefore, the only requests that I ask of my students are a daily spiritual exercise of thirty minutes and to employ moderation in all things while living the spiritual life, whether through the physical, emotional, mental, or spiritual senses.

26. **Q**. Could you explain just what the requirements are for being accepted as one of your students?

A. I require a stable mind, coupled with a deep desire and yearning to discover both your truest self and your ultimate Source. And of course, I also ask that you send me a letter expressing these same sentiments and requesting to become a student. But in truth, I do not require anything, as I am simply carrying out Anami's divine will. Anami is an Ocean of Love and Bliss and only asks that we yearn more for the Creator than the creation, that we yearn for the self and God above all else. When an individual finds oneself within this level of sincerity, this state of consciousness, one is qualified, and this is all the Lord asks of us. To desire the true self and God over and above the created universe is an achievement that few have attained. It is rather easy for the ego to presume that it would choose Heaven over earth in a heartbeat, but this is the exception rather than the rule. The conscious ego so loves its present desires that to even consider desiring God more than them is simply a nuisance and an inconvenient consideration for the ego. Generally speaking, most people are content in their unhappy condition and would not exchange their lives for another's, nor would they desire a higher level of existence even if it were offered to them.

Lord Krishna, in his parable of the pig, made this very point to one of his disgruntled disciples, and it so infuriated this man that he wanted desperately to prove Lord Krishna wrong. Lord Krishna had simply been asked why he did not lift up those souls immediately around him, and he had replied that it was because they would not be eager to leave this world and go to a higher Heaven. Lord Krishna then told this disciple that if he could find any creature that did want to ascend to the next higher level, to bring that creature to him and it would be done. So the man began running around the countryside looking for any creature he could find, and he finally came across a pig. The disciple told the pig that he would be granted a higher level of existence if he would only come before Lord Krishna and ask to be lifted into the world of heavenly consciousness. The pig, considering himself an academic, replied, "I am not as gullible as I might appear, and I will not be taken for a fool. I have some questions to ask first."

The pig then inquired of the disciple about the conditions of this higher level, and the disciple replied, "The higher region is spotlessly clean with many lovely fragrances." The pig appeared skeptical and, with beady eyes, asked another question, "Will there be muddied straw and dung for me to roll and sleep in?" The disciple retorted, "Heaven does not contain such filth." "Aha, just as I thought," replied the pig, "Such a place might be Heaven to a fool like you, but to me, the place you are describing sounds more like hell."

It is extremely difficult for the mind to imagine that the next higher level above it could be better than its present station, and thus it remains reluctant to relinquish its current reality, even when offered the promise of a higher existence. This is what makes truth seekers so uniquely different, for they are brimming with zeal and are consciously willing to transition themselves to the next higher level. This parable also magnificently reveals that no matter what the disgruntled disciple did, he could not prove Lord Krishna wrong. The disciple was projecting and transferring his own frustration onto the Master and the pig, but in truth, he was only angry with himself, for he was refusing the help meant for him, thereby preventing himself from being lifted into a higher existence. None are so blind as those who refuse to see.

27. **Q.** It seems to me that the whole world is filled with angry people lashing out at one another these days. So many are voicing negative criticism toward differing spiritual methodologies, and there is a ton of guru bashing and a host of other hostile reactions all over the Internet.

There just seems to be a visible dissension toward all things spiritual, and I was wondering how you view the many detractors and angry critics in the world today?

A. This is a good question, and it is one that many other spiritual seekers have both considered and anguished over. But in truth, we must be realistic about all of the opposition within the world, for it is prevalent in all quarters, not just in the religious or spiritual arenas. There are constant conflicts between husbands and wives, children and parents, morality and immorality, good and bad, positive and negative, democrats and republicans, and between one belief and another. All of this simply points to the raging conflict between the opposing forces of duality.

We live in a dual world, and everything within it has a distinct opposite, a direct polarity, all for the purpose of maintaining a workable balance in all realms of the creation. Humankind is not sufficiently evolved to the point where each and every person can induce a balanced response to the experiences they encounter, and so the overall "dual life force" must administer this balance upon the world and those who inhabit it. Rather than being overly sensitive when viewing all of this and seeing it as unpardonable, unnecessary, or even as an unbearable burden to shoulder, it should simply be viewed as inevitable, for it is part and parcel of our ephemeral and warring universe.

There will always be individuals who are either for or against, partial or impartial, and they will relate to their own point of view as the highest of all, freely passing judgment on others and asserting themselves in ways that are perfectly acceptable to them, although not to others. Detractors come in all shapes and sizes: Some are disgruntled former students of various paths; some are religious zealots who are offended that their own unique belief system is not universally accepted; others are deprogrammers, who are really twenty-first century gunslingers; and still others are even wayward initiates from one of the Light and Sound Paths present in the world today.

My advice is to let detractors be detractors, for their experience is just as important to them as our experience is to us. Every individual is right in one's own eyes, and each will ultimately be judged for one's own actions, just like you and I will be. If you deny them their right to be as they wish, you risk forfeiting your own spirituality, and you should not compromise yourself in this fashion. I would suggest penetrating and transcending your own overly sensitive nature by growing a thicker skin. Practice detachment and learn to laugh off all opposition, for in truth, not everyone can be in agreement with your point of view.

The Light and Sound Teachings represent a controversial message, for it goes against the traditional beliefs of the world, it bucks the status quo of the bulk of humanity, and it can even openly challenge or confront the formative conditioning most people were imprinted with in their youth. Furthermore, since you cannot control what other people think or say, you should not be overly concerned about it. Focus only on those things you can control, always remembering that censorship and ridicule serve as the guards to the market of love. It is unbecoming of any Light and Sound Master, as well as His students, to take issue with or to speak ill of anyone, even though in truth, all Saints and Masters in past and present times have had their living Judas. And similarly, the world has never been kind to the Saints and their disciples. It is far better to understand and deftly rise above the mechanical nature of the human mind operating within the duality of the earthly world, than it is to mentally agonize or become emotionally upset by it.

28. **Q.** I have heard you speak of illumination, enlightenment, and an expansion of consciousness, and I am curious to know how these higher levels are achieved. Does it just involve study of your books and recordings, like in college, or do you simply wake up in the morning and find these greater truths suddenly present? Or maybe dreams or visions play a part? I'm just not sure, so could you explain further?

A. Thank you, and I certainly get the drift of your questions. You have actually answered your own inquiry, because you have unknowingly just expressed the four mediums that are used to transfer this higher consciousness to the individual student. Contemplation of the Light and Sound doctrine, spontaneous revelations, dreams, and visions are the primary modalities used to infuse and impregnate our own human consciousness with this all-encompassing Sound Current. I use the words "medium" and "modality" to describe these practices, for without the Sound Current that flows through these passageways, these very same practices would be nothing other than empty shells lacking the true kernel. This is the essential difference between the Light and Sound approach and other endeavors, that is, the essence of the Sound Current versus the essence of the universal mind power. All techniques are for the mind, whether prayer, meditation, or contemplation, and in the majority of cases, only the universal mind power is invoked. When an initiate of the Light and Sound employs these same practices or techniques, it is the Sound Current that rushes through rather than the universal mind power, and the difference in results is dramatic and life changing.

Eighty-five percent of the spiritual instruction on the MasterPath is conducted and imparted on the inner planes of consciousness, and this ability to impart the Teachings on both the outer and inner planes is one of the major earmarks of a true Master, or Saint. The Dream Master rendezvous nightly with the initiates, whether they are aware of it or not, and together they explore and make ingress into the students' own higher worlds of consciousness. The Dream Master appears just as the Outer Master does and so easy recognition is possible. Normal dreaming is simply an extension of our daily waking life, but spiritual dreams are actual visitations to other, higher dimensions.

29. **Q**. I am somewhat confused about the different Faces of the Master. Is the Dream Master the same as the Inner Master?

A. Yes and no. I must say "no" because the primary objective of both the Outer Master and the Dream Master is only to assist the students in collecting and centering their soul currents back into the third eye. But upon entering this aperture, the Radiant Form of the Inner Master is experienced for the first time. Therefore, all three of these forms of the Master, the Outer Master, the Dream Master, and the Inner Master, are uniquely different, and each has a specific mission to perform.

The reason I also answered "yes" to your question is because even though there are multiple manifestations of the majestic Sound Current and each is distinctly different, they are all comprised of the exact same Essence. All of the separate forms of the Master are comprised of and represent varying intensities, or grades, of this all-pervasive Sound Current. Each of them is a separate representation of the same Sound Current manifesting Itself distinctively on each descending plane. So in truth, the various Faces of the Master are solely comprised of the same spiritual Essence, although each has a unique spiritual responsibility to fulfill.

This is actually the essential explanation of why the Light and Sound Teachings do not fall into the realm or definition of cultic practice, for the pure spiritual Sound Current is the true Master, and this omnipresent Current emanating from God embodies and comprises all of the varying manifestations of the Master, whether the Outer, Dream, or Inner Master. The sole mission of these three Faces of the Master is to awaken you to your own internal Sound Current, the Spirit within you, thereby allowing the journey of soul to begin.

30. **Q**. I have been seeking a true Master for decades, and I must admit that I expected a Sat Guru to look different, more like the ancient adepts I have seen from the Far East. Is this just a surface distinction or are there real differences between Masters from the East and a Western Sat Guru?

A. That's a great question, and I am happy to respond. Yes indeed, you are observing and investigating an American Sat Guru, and I do not wear a turban, I do not have a beard, and I do not don a white robe. This raises a very pertinent question. What do you expect the Master to be? How do you expect Him to look? We all have an image of what we expect a Master to be, but America and the West are seeing a Sat Guru here in the twenty-first century, and He is not an Indian Guru. Thus, please allow me to first address the issue of cultural differences. When we incarnate into a new lifetime, we are born into a certain country, a particular family, and a specific culture. We are given ways to view and are literally conditioned in how to think and live with all of our fellow citizens within our country of origin. Let us say that this country is America. So, as an

American, we will learn the ways of American culture, including the heightened degrees of selfishness, desire, and capitalistic yearning for possessions that abound in this country. But when we have outgrown the cultural norm, what are we to do? In the past, when anyone had reached the zenith of their spiritual pursuit in this country, where did they have to go to find more? They had to go to India or some other country in the East. That is predominantly where the Light and Sound Masters have been for thousands of years. America is a very, very young country. It has been establishing its own government, its own conscience, and its own consciousness, and the need has now arisen for an American Sat Guru, a Master who has a unique type of appeal to the Western consciousness and culture.

When a Westerner who wants to pursue Sound goes to India and begins practicing under the tutelage of an Indian Master, they often, though not always, experience certain difficulties. The primary difficulty is that the Indian Master was raised within India's culture, and much of India's ways of thinking and ways of life are very different from our experience in the West. Several of the largest Light and Sound Paths in the East are over one hundred years old, and their roots go back much further yet. These Paths were fashioned by past Masters to fit and serve the needs of individuals living in that particular culture and time period. Therefore, if you were to go to India and seek initiation into the Sound Current from a Master there, you would find their methods of presenting the Teachings and their required disciplines, or vows, very different from those of MasterPath, although the Teachings, the principles themselves, would essentially be the same.

Generally, the Light and Sound Masters in India recommend two and one-half hours of meditation every day. The students are required to assume a rather strict vegetarian diet. Alcohol, drugs, and tobacco are staunchly forbidden. Celibacy is required outside of marriage. And most of the major Paths assume that the disciples will donate at least ten percent of their total income to the Path. I say all of this very respectfully, and there is absolutely no put-down being conveyed. And similarly, if a student from a very traditional environment in the East came here to the West and took up the Path here, he or she would experience these types of culture-based difficulties as well. It is not absolutely necessary to be taught or initiated by a Master from the same cultural background as your own, but many students find it to be simply more harmonious.

There are tremendous advantages for a Westerner having a Western Master. If your chosen Master has the same cultural background as you do, He will have had many similar experiences to your own. He will have had the same good times, as well as the hard times, and He will more easily be able to assist you in unraveling many of the cultural influences and impressions that you have been stamped with. No Sat Guru can alter or change the Teachings, but each one is responsible for establishing current policies within the particular culture they are serving. My concern is not what will appeal to the people in the West, but which policies, requirements, and spiritual disciplines will most harmoniously benefit those students who are living in this culture.

Therefore, I simply ask my students to engage in their spiritual practice for approximately twenty to thirty minutes a day, and I ask that they practice the Presence of the Master as they go through their daily lives. I have seen far too many students who have attempted the two and one-half hour practice recommended by most Eastern Light and Sound Masters, and they are guilt-ridden because of their inability to adhere to this discipline. I feel the shorter spiritual exercise actually yields better results for Westerners, given their mental makeup, their attention span, and the time constraints of their active lifestyles. As the Western culture changes, of course, the disciplines will again change as well, for the time will come when the language, dress, and lifestyle of our present culture evolves to the point where it is nearly unrecognizable to the citizens of today. And likewise, whoever the Sat Guru may be at that time will then have to assess the culture and the collective consciousness and alter the policies and requirements accordingly.

I set no dietary requirements for my students, but I do urge them to take proper care of their physical bodies. I have no issue with an occasional social drink, as long as my students are not dependent upon alcohol or any other mind-altering substance. The sweet elixir that is the Sound Current, or the Shabda, does not mix well with such excesses. However, rather than vows of total abstinence, I ask my students to create balance in their individual lives. This applies not only to food, alcohol, recreational drugs, or sexual activity, but also to all life, whether work and leisure, sleep and activity, or even the giving and receiving of the Spirit.

There is no way that anyone can permanently relinquish one's imbalance or lack of moderation, one's attachments and crutches, without first replacing them with something greater. Until you get the divine Sound Current roaring through your veins, this is nearly impossible to do. One of the most successful techniques of the negative power within you involves its effort to get you to believe that you must quit a certain behavior before you can be a spiritual person. The individual then applies all kinds of personal will and great mental effort to the task, conveniently forgetting the Master's help. This is because most students are usually so ashamed of such behavior that they refuse to let the Master into these areas of their lives. However, in truth, the Master loves each soul far more than one could ever hate one's own defilements. Thus, the Master will help each of His students to slowly but surely fall in love with and learn to fully access one's own Sound Current. And as one does, all remaining attachments and excesses naturally come into balance over time or they just vanish entirely.

All true Masters teach one and the same truth: The true Path was indelibly imprinted within each soul's consciousness before any outer Path was even created. The true way back to the Divine Deity is through our own consciousness. God designed it this way, for even before we had a human body, the spiritual Path was etched within our consciousness, our own immortal soul. The purpose of the true Path and Master is simply to help you first discover and then embark upon this divine journey, which will ultimately deliver you straightway into your own liberation, realization, and eternal salvation in soul.

For further information,
please contact:

MasterPath
P.O. Box 9035
Temecula, CA 92589

www.masterpath.org

GLOSSARY

—A—

ABSOLUTE TRUTH – The unified essence of the Shabda; the all-inclusive truth, in contrast to relative truth that is divided into fragmented parts (duality); must be caught with the subtle spiritual senses and cannot be taught or experienced intellectually.

AGAM LOK – Seventh level of Heaven.

ALAKH LOK – Sixth level of Heaven.

ANAMI LOK – Eighth level of Heaven.

ANAMI PURUSH – See: *GOD*.

ANGER – One of the five passions of the mind; manifests in reaction to an unfulfilled desire.

ASCENDED MASTER – Any Master or Saint who has translated (physical death) such as Jesus, Nanak, Hafiz, Kabir, Rumi, and Sawan Singh Ji; a teacher of any level of awareness who does not have a physical body; cannot initiate soul into the Sound Current, as only a Living Master carries the power of initiation.

ASTRAL PLANE – First level of Heaven; region of more refined and subtle energies than the physical plane; the realm of romanticized psychic phenomena and emotionalism; origin of the prana energies; houses numerous Heavens of various religions.

ASTRAL PROJECTION – Psychic phenomenon in which the astral body splits from the physical body to travel only as far as the astral plane; discouraged by true Masters as a limited and potentially dangerous practice.

ATTACHMENT – One of the five passions of the mind; bonds one to both positive and negative images, concepts, and emotional experiences through an inclination to possess.

ATTENTION – One of the four fundamental principles of spirituality (attention, attitude, discrimination, detachment); a manifestation of soul's energy; an externalized expression of soul; when unmonitored, used by mind to move downward and outward, ensuring separation from the Divine; pivotal aspect and function of the spiritual exercise.

ATTITUDE – One of the four fundamental principles of spirituality (attention, attitude, discrimination, detachment); a manifestation of soul's energy; quality of emotional feeling that determines how something is viewed and how one identifies with an experience (downward and outward versus inward and upward).

—B—

BEING, BEINGNESS – Attribute of the realized soul; a spiritual naturalness, devoid of lower self-concern.

BHAKTI – Soul's innate love and devotion.

BHANWAR GUPHA – Fourth level of Heaven.

BODY CONSCIOUSNESS – Level of diffused spiritual energy that keeps soul's attention trapped in concerns of the physical body.

BRAHM – The ruling power of the lower three worlds; Lord God to the traditional religions; all lower world functions are regulated by this universal mind power; the origin of mind.

—C—

CAUSAL PLANE – Division of the second level of Heaven; storehouse for records of past lives.

CAUSE AND EFFECT – Ruling principle of the lower worlds; for every action (cause), there is an equal and opposite reaction (effect). See: KARMA.

CHAKRAS – Energy centers, or plexuses, within the five-bodied human entity; serve to regulate all physical, emotional, mental, and spiritual functions.

CHELA – Initiate, student, disciple of a Living Master; one who associates with truth's reality; soul is the chela, not mind, ego, or personality.

CHRIST CONSCIOUSNESS – A traditional religious title; esoterically, the Christ consciousness is equal to the cosmic consciousness in the realms of Trikuti.

CONSCIOUS MIND – Physical mind; lowest of the three minds (conscious, subconscious, unconscious); exclusively concerned with external reality in day-to-day functions.

CONSCIOUSNESS – Soul; attention; innate quality of soul that gives life and vitality to all bodies, chakras, and realms of creation; expressed as awareness.

CONTEMPLATION – One of the four primary methods of petitioning the Divine (prayer, meditation, contemplation, soul transport); a spiritual exercise; unrestrained examination of any spiritual ideal and its application to one's individual experience; recommended procedure which facilitates the emancipation of consciousness; gives purpose to the focusing of attention upon a spiritual principle, ideal, or the Presence of the Master; incorporates and directs the mind, while discovering, extracting, awakening, and purifying the attention faculty.

COSMIC CONSCIOUSNESS – Enlightenment in the divine mind; harmonizing the three minds (conscious, subconscious, unconscious); pinnacle of the universal mind power.

CRUCIFIXION – Esoteric process of conscious purification, wherein the initiated soul ascends in consciousness to escape the encumbrance of the lower pinda mind; ultimately precedes entry into the third eye; total sacrifice of lower realities for higher spiritual truths.

CULT – Outwardly manifests as a group consciousness worshiping a charismatic personality who manipulates the energies of the followers; inwardly manifests as ego and personality.

—D—

DASWAN DWAR – Third level of Heaven.

DEATH – Esoterically, the spiritual process of soul withdrawing its sensory currents (attention) inward and upward, and establishing them in the third eye; dying while living is the gateway to eternal life. See: *TRANSLATION; CRUCIFIXION.*

DETACHMENT – One of the four fundamental principles of spirituality (attention, attitude, discrimination, detachment);

the active spiritual state of compassionate neutrality; distinctly different than renunciation or expressions of asceticism.

DEVOLUTION – Soul's experience of descending into the lower worlds and taking on bodies (soul, mental, causal, astral, physical) in order to gather the experiences necessary for its later ascent via evolution.

DHARAM RAI – Karmic judge; assesses both positive and negative karma and administers reward and/or punishment at the physical death of the uninitiated soul; only the Master and His chela bypass the court of Dharam Rai, as the Master escorts each chela from the physical body upon translation.

DISCIPLE – Soul; chela of a true Master.

DISCRIMINATION – One of the four fundamental principles of spirituality (attention, attitude, detachment, discrimination); open inquiry and careful study; separating the real from the unreal, truth from untruth.

DIVINE INHERITANCE – Birthright of soul to fully mature its consciousness and realize its power to create and fulfill the entire purpose of life and all creation.

DIVINE MIND – Unconscious, or universal, mind; the highest of the three minds (conscious, subconscious, unconscious); the most subtle form of the universal mind power, more pure than the conscious and subconscious minds; its highest attainment is cosmic consciousness.

DIVINE WILL – Supreme intention and pure desire of God; purposeful design of the Absolute that purely serves the devolution, evolution, and spiritual unfoldment of all life, in contrast to the personal will that serves only the satisfaction of the body, emotions, mind, ego, and personality.

DREAM MASTER – Inner Form of the Outer Master who works with the student in consciousness beneath the eye center to bring increased understanding of the Outer Master's Teachings and their personal application; serves as a bridge leading from the Outer Master to the Radiant Form of the Master.

DUALITY, DUAL WORLDS – Lower universe consisting of matter, energy, space, and time; yin and yang; positive and negative; all within the dual worlds must have an opposite in order to exist.

— **E** —

EGO – The false self; manifestation of the universal mind power; the essence of separation from soul, Spirit, and God; promotes separation by viewing all experiences through the lens of I, me, and mine; lives as if duality were truth and is blindly attached to being right.

EL CAMINO REAL – Literally, royal road; circulates the Shabda Dhun; the central channel in the subtle body, immediately beyond the third eye center; discovered and traversed by means of spiritual practice according to the instructions of a Sat Guru; leads one to the divine Origin; also known as the narrow way, middle road, royal vein, and grand trunk road.

ELIMINATION CHAKRA – First and lowest chakra in the physical body; will power is developed, allowing one to fulfill worldly obligations and mundane duties.

EMANCIPATION – First level of Self Realization; freedom from the passions of the mind and karma.

EMOTION – The language of the astral body subject to the limited viewpoints of the subconscious mind; gives vitality to thought; expresses itself through the heart chakra in the body consciousness.

ENERGY – In the macrocosm, the reflection of the Divine's essence brought down into the lower creation as form; in the microcosm, the reflection of soul's essence as attitude and attention.

ENLIGHTENMENT – Relative attainment of harmonizing the three minds with the universal mind power. See: *COSMIC CONSCIOUSNESS*.

ESOTERICISM – Inner mystical truth and reality imparted by a Living Master and known only to His initiates; beyond duality; secret; the Light and Sound Teachings, which explain Anami's creation and soul's journey Home through the inner worlds in consciousness.

EXOTERICISM – Reflection, or shadow, of esotericism; relative truth; manifestation of duality and form; impermanent, yet appearing to be eternal; promotes all modes of self-improvement, in contrast to self-discovery.

EYE OF SOUL – See: *THIRD EYE*.

—**F**—

FATE KARMA – One's destiny in life, created by actions in one or more previous lives, and upon which one's present life is based.

—**G**—

GOD – Anami Purush, which literally means Nameless Power; Supreme Creator and ultimate reality; the unmanifest; omniscient, formless, omnipotent, and ubiquitous; the Creator of all life, soul, love, truth, and wisdom.

GOD REALIZATION – Total absorption into the divine self; perfection of one's own soul; beingness of a fully matured soul in oneness with the Divine.

GOLDEN CHAINS – Bonds of karma created and sustained through attraction to the positive aspects of human consciousness, such as personal love, helping others, or attachment to worldly pleasures; refers to what most humans consider great fortune, good luck, and seemingly ideal or positive circumstances. See: *IRON SHACKLES*.

GREED – One of the five passions of the mind; impulsive drive to amass possessions and the attempt to acquire peace, love, and tranquility through the manipulation of outer conditions.

GURU – Spiritual teacher; master; adept; guide; a Sat Guru brings the Sound Current as the liberating power, and a pseudo guru brings knowledge, or light; origin in Sanskrit, "gu" means destroyer, and "ru" means darkness.

—**H**—

HEART CHAKRA – Fourth chakra in the physical body; represents the focus of one's emotional love and attachment to outer concerns; seat of religious paths.

HEAVEN – Esoterically, eight distinct regions of consciousness within each individual; the level of spiritual attainment that determines the specific level of consciousness in which one resides; the consciousness of God within soul; the origin of soul; exoterically, a reward of paradise outside of oneself, only accessible after death if religious codes have been followed.

HIGHER SELF – See: *SOUL.*

HUMAN CONSCIOUSNESS – Soul energy trapped in the lower body chakras and ruled completely by karma and the five passions of the mind; seeks to acquire love, truth, and peace outwardly.

—**I**—

ILLUMINATION – Level of consciousness that is experienced in the astral plane, through association and merging with the Radiant Form of the Master.

ILLUSION – Deception; manifests subjectively through an internal assumption based in untruth.

INITIATION – Re-awakening of soul and the Audible Life Stream via the Sat Guru; gateway to the mysteries of Anami Purush.

INNER MASTER – See: *SAT GURU AS THE INNER MASTER.*

IRON SHACKLES – Bonds of karma created by attraction to the negative aspects of human consciousness and experience; examples include but are not limited to greed, anger, lust, vanity, attachment, fear, hatred, and violence. See: *GOLDEN CHAINS.*

—**J**—

JESUS – Master of the Light and Sound Teachings; a Param Saint; revealed the esoteric secrets of the Sound Current to His initiated chelas; His teachings were misunderstood and turned into an exoteric religion; was recognized by His predecessor, John the Baptist, who initiated Him.

JOURNEY OF SOUL – The incomprehensibly vast devolution and evolution of soul's maturation in consciousness.

—K—

KARMA – The law of cause and effect, or action and reaction; the power that drives reincarnation, entrapping soul in the cycle of birth and death; a method of remedial training that serves the maturation of soul; described in the biblical references "as you sow, so shall you reap" and "an eye for an eye"; contemporarily voiced as "what goes around, comes around."

KUNDALINI – Motor currents; concentration of the prana energies stored at the base of the spine; associated with the powers of the elimination and reproductive chakras; chelas leave this energy untouched.

—L—

LAW OF CAUSE AND EFFECT – See: *KARMA; CAUSE AND EFFECT.*

LEVELS OF CONSCIOUSNESS – Stages of soul's maturation and purification experienced as it ascends into its Godhood: the body chakras, third eye, cosmic consciousness, Self Realization, Spiritual Realization, and God Realization.

LIBERATION – The essential emancipation of consciousness from the lower bodies; soul is free from the tyranny of the physical, astral, causal, and mental bodies.

LIFE FORCE – Universally, the Essence of Shabda; individually, the essence of soul.

LIGHT – One of the two attributes of Anami Purush (Light and Sound) used to create and sustain all life; unitary, undifferentiated essence of Spirit as it descends through Anami's creation before reaching the mental plane; upon reaching the mental plane, light is diffused and divided into the streams of duality; diffused, it is the essence of the universal mind power, which reveals the contents of the mind through reason, logic, and the psychic senses and cannot deliver soul to Self Realization; all must go through the light (mind) to get to the Sound (soul).

LIGHT AND SOUND PATH, LIGHT AND SOUND TEACHINGS – The imprint of Anami as the inner Path indelibly etched in the heart of every soul; indwelling Path revealed by the Living Master that leads soul to its Home in the Divine; the outer instruction that gives form to the inner, unwritten law and unspoken language, the true Word of Anami's essence; the God-made Path in contrast to paths invented by humankind. See: *MASTERPATH; SURAT SHABDA YOGA*.

LIGHT GURU, OR MASTER – See: *PSEUDO GURU*.

LIVING MASTER – See: *SAT GURU AS THE OUTER MASTER*.

LOWER SELF – See: *MIND/EGO COMPLEX*.

LOWER WORLDS – Lower three planes (physical, astral, and mental), where duality reigns and karma locks one onto the wheel of eighty-four; training ground for soul to develop spiritual readiness and to meet and begin unfoldment through a living Sat Guru.

LUST – One of the five passions of the mind; drives all types of excessive appetites which seek to indulge in the pleasure principle; self-indulgence.

—M—

MACROCOSM – The body of the Divine Creator; the entirety of creation including all regions and levels of consciousness;

encompasses soul's journey through devolution and evolution to fulfill the purpose of creation; reflected within each individual as the microcosm.

MASTER – A true Master, or Saint, is one who has attained God Realization and channels the Light and Sound, as opposed to a master of light, who channels the universal mind power.

MASTERPATH – Contemporary expression of the ancient Teachings of Light and Sound, of Surat Shabda Yoga, and Anami's Path back to Itself, which is tailored for the Western culture; upholds the sanctity of the Original Teachings while moderating traditional Eastern vows; objective is to lead soul back to its own innate Mastership; expression of the divine principle that the chela is the eventual Master, and the Path to the Lord's Kingdom lies within each soul; emphasizes contemplation versus meditation, accelerating the conscious emancipation of soul; founded by Sri Gary Olsen in 1987.

MASTERS OF LIGHT AND SOUND – Souls who have achieved God Realization, and who are appointed by the Supreme Creator to manifest into a human body to serve as vehicles for the divine dispensation of the Sound Current.

MASTERSHIP – Sainthood; God Realization is established.

MAYA – Delusion within the body consciousness; unreality; conscious mind's way of perceiving life; all that is not real and true; entraps soul energies in the body chakras through deception and distortion of truth; manipulates one's perceptions of external conditions, convincing one they are real and true.

MECHANICAL EVOLUTION – The progression of soul's unfoldment through the mineral, plant, reptile, animal, and human experiences via the universal mind power, without the assistance of the inherent Sound Current; means by which soul experiences varying levels of relative truth (light) in preparation for spiritual evolution, which begins upon initiation by a true Living Master. See: SPIRITUAL EVOLUTION.

MEDITATION – One of the four primary methods of petitioning the Divine (prayer, meditation, contemplation, soul transport); the practice of attempting to still the lower mind with the higher mind; established by past Light and Sound Masters and is specifically tailored to address Eastern conditions, mindset, and cultural context; has been replaced by contemplation as the recommended spiritual practice in the contemporary Western expression of the Light and Sound Teachings.

MENTAL PLANE – Division of the second level of Heaven; home of the universal mind power, which creates knowledge, thought, reason, logic, intellect, speculation, factoids, concepts, perception, and information.

MENTAL SENSES – Thought, volition, reason, logic, philosophy, conjecture, speculation, and theory; expressions of the lower and higher minds.

METAPHYSICS – Psychic sciences that explore the physical, astral, causal, and mental planes.

MICROCOSM – Individualized macrocosm placed within each human body; microcosmic centers within the bodies that exactly reflect the macrocosmic centers; all living beings within creation have within themselves a microcosm of the macrocosm; Kingdom of Heaven is within one's own microcosm.

MIND – Repository of universal mind power in the individual; designed to encumber the soul in its devolution into the lower worlds; expressed as the conscious, subconscious, and unconscious minds; must be spiritualized through soul's intimate association with a true and Living Master.

MIND/EGO COMPLEX – Lower constitution that rules all physical, emotional, and mental identities void of soul, Sound, and the Sat Guru; counterpart to soul that creates and sustains all attachments to relative truth and light.

MORALISM – Rigid code that exemplifies the universal mind power and dictates thought, feeling, and behavior; attempts to control a singular aspect of duality by imposing rights and wrongs, do's and don'ts; holds self-improvement as an exalted spiritual method; necessary stage in mechanical evolution.

MOTOR CURRENTS – Energies within the human body; currents that are indigenous to the universal mind power; not used by the chela, as the Master instructs one to exclusively concentrate the sensory currents.

—**N**—

NAVEL CHAKRA – Third chakra in the physical body; governs how one nourishes oneself, including food, prestige, desires, etc.

—**O**—

OCEAN OF LOVE AND MERCY – Anami Purush; Home of truth and the divine origin of soul; indescribable reality of soul experiencing union with the Master, the Shabda, and ultimately, Anami Purush; soul is the drop from this Ocean of the Divine.

ORIGINAL SIN – Esoterically, refers to the origin of one's own distortion of truth that created the separation from the One into many; exoterically, the illusion of an inherent blemish in soul; religious doctrine that promotes unworthiness and distorts or hides the original purity of soul.

OUTER MASTER – See: *SAT GURU AS THE OUTER MASTER*.

—**P**—

PARAM SAINT – Natural-born Saint; Swateh Saint; founding Saint; the first Master in a new line, who re-enters the world to re-establish purity of truth and Sound in a fresh, contemporary manner.

PASSIONS OF THE MIND – Anger, lust, greed, attachment, and vanity; traits of the universal mind power which are imprinted in the three minds of all humans; promote and sustain mind's identification with external conditions.

PERCEPTION – A primary function of soul; one's angle of vision determined by one's state of consciousness; determines one's reality; mind only reflects the perceptive power of soul.

PERSONAL WILL – Unconscious promotion of karmic tendencies; expressions of the personality and ego; the signature of arrogant vanity; thinking, feeling, and discriminating on behalf of the lower bodies; serves the false self. See: *DIVINE WILL*.

PERSONALITY – The expression of individual karmic style; the personal reaction to one's conditioning made into habitual expressions.

PHILOSOPHY – An expression of the universal mind power that arouses the mental energies in order to intellectualize existence.

PHYSICAL BODY – Coarsest covering of the incarnated soul; limited to experiences in the physical plane, or outer world;

has five senses and is subject to the physical laws of the universe, including birth and death; houses the four more subtle bodies (astral, causal, mental, and soul).

PHYSICAL CONSCIOUSNESS – See: *BODY CONSCIOUSNESS.*

PHYSICAL PLANE – Lowest plane in the macrocosm, wherein soul is encumbered by mental, emotional, and physical senses within the physical body.

PHYSICAL SENSES – The body senses that allow soul to gather experiences on the physical plane in the body consciousness.

PINDA PLANE – See: *PHYSICAL PLANE.*

PRANA – Vital force; manifestations of the motor currents; sourced in the astral plane.

PRAYER – One of the four primary methods of petitioning the Divine (prayer, meditation, contemplation, soul transport); requesting the divine assistance of the unconscious mind to resolve a subconscious problem that the conscious mind cannot transcend due to its limited reason.

PROVISIONAL FAITH – Faith that is flexible and alive, in contrast to blind faith; willingness to act on one's own spiritual behalf by investigating the Master and His Teachings, being aware of one's yearning for truth and fear of exploitation, honestly assessing one's changes in consciousness, and taking another step in the process; acting to know.

PSEUDO GURU – Master of light; one who channels the universal mind power; promotes the light of relative truth for souls who are developing through mechanical evolution; a teacher who has not yet realized soul or the Sound; self-appointed guru.

PSYCHIC PRACTICES – All expressions of the light, including astrology, ESP, tarot, hypnosis, meditation, prophecy, astral projection, I Ching, psychic readings, religion, shamanistic rituals, drumming, past-life regressions, aura adjustments, mediumship, and visions; all attempts to manipulate the forces of duality to temporarily change outer conditions.

PSYCHIC WORLDS – Technically, all creation beneath Sat Lok; entered in any moment of separation from soul, Sound, and the Sat Guru.

—R—

RADIANT FORM OF THE MASTER – The Outer Master's inner radiant form; works with the chela on the inner planes; manifests to the initiate in the astral plane (the esoteric second coming); called the Glorified Body in the Bible. See: RENDEZVOUS WITH THE RADIANT FORM OF THE MASTER.

READINESS – Condition of a soul that has ascended through experiences within the physical plane, now ready to be initiated into God's system of returning Home through the tutelage, protection, and love of a Living Master.

REINCARNATION – The cycles of birth and death required to address one's karma, which is the remedial education of soul; the mechanism that cultivates spiritual readiness, gracing entrapped souls the opportunity to meet a Living Master and receive initiation; the movement of the wheel of eighty-four that eventually drives soul into seeking truth everlasting.

RELATIVE TRUTH – All that exists beneath Sat Lok; inherently dualistic, capable of reflecting only partial aspects of absolute truth; void of the absolute unifying power of Sound; Anami's principle of perfection that allows degrees of truth and love to be experienced by soul, regardless of level of devolvement or evolvement.

RELIGION – An exoteric reflection of esoteric mysticism void of a living Godman, who is needed to reveal the inner Way; relative expression of the universal mind power (light) within the physical, astral, and causal planes; develops relative degrees of devotion and surrender, allowing soul to unfold through natural evolution.

RENDEZVOUS WITH THE RADIANT FORM OF THE MASTER – Esoteric experience of the second coming, wherein the chela's surat, or attention, rises above body consciousness and encounters the Radiant Form of the Master within.

REPRODUCTIVE CHAKRA – Second chakra in the physical body; source of creative energy for the unenlightened soul seeking union with objects and persons in the outside world; responsible for procreation in the physical world.

—S—

SAINT – Esoterically, one who has reached the fifth spiritual region and has realized the Supreme Creator; one who is empowered to ignite the Sound Current within devotees through the sacred rite of initiation; redeems soul in true salvation.

SALVATION – God Realization; must be achieved while in the physical incarnation; essential promise of initiation from a Sat Guru.

SANT MAT – Teachings of the Saints promulgated by Eastern Light and Sound Masters.

SAT – True beingness.

SAT GURU AS THE INNER MASTER – The truc Guru is the Sound Current, or the melodious and eternal Voice of Anami; formless, eternal and omnipresent, omnipotent, and omniscient; it is this Sound Current that manifests all forms of the five-bodied complex of the Master; all worship is directed toward this Inner Sound; the Outer Sat Guru reconnects the soul to this Sound Current; Shabda is the Sat Guru, and the Outer Master is Its lesser form.

SAT GURU AS THE OUTER MASTER – True Master; true Teacher, Master Soul, spiritual adept; Living Master, who brings the pure, positive Light of the Divine into the darkness of the lower worlds; a Saint who is a spiritual wayshower, adept at initiating all levels of soul's unfoldment into Self, Spirit, and God Realization; the ultimate spiritual being; indispensable, for He enlivens the true Teachings, embodies the true Name, and serves as the Divine's true representative in all of creation; the Beloved, the Friend, the Comforter, the Son of God; lives in the hearts of those who love Him; every true Master or Sat Guru is a Saint, but not all Saints are Sat Gurus.

SAT LOK – Fifth level of Heaven.

SEEKER – One who searches for the essence of Spirit, soul, and the deeper purpose of life; one who is sincerely yearning for truth.

SELF-DISCIPLINE – Conscious control of the lower self; continuously monitoring the placement of attention and the quality of one's attitude; control of the emotions and imagination; distinctly different than denial or renunciation.

SELF REALIZATION – Esoteric experience of soul recognizing itself, liberated from the confines of the lower self (mind, ego, personality).

SENSORY CURRENTS – The higher currents of attention, consciousness, and soul energy; enliven and sustain the higher bodies, while in contrast, the motor currents operate and sustain the physical body.

SENSORY-INTELLECTUAL CONSCIOUSNESS – Consciousness that is associated with all physical and mental expressions and impressions beneath the third eye.

SHABDA – See: SOUND CURRENT.

SIN – A religious construct that promotes the belief that soul is impure; ancient Greek archery term meaning missing the mark; distorted concept of the universal mind power, which engenders fear, guilt, and repression.

SINCERITY – Soul attribute that hinges on the appreciation for truth and one's genuine yearning to emancipate consciousness from bondage; soul quality that attracts the Master to one; a key ingredient to consciously recognize the need for a Living Master.

SOUL – Surat; attention; consciousness; one's true essence and identity; a unit of awareness; a drop from the divine Ocean of Love and Mercy; the eternal spark of formless being; gives life to the lower four bodies and makes their functions dynamic; the only vehicle that can rise above the worlds of duality; a happy and blissful entity.

SOUL CONSCIOUSNESS – Spontaneous awareness and direct perception.

SOUL PLANE – Regions of pure, unalloyed bliss and concentrated Spirit; reality of purity, God Realization, release from the wheel of eighty-four, and freedom from the five passions.

SOUND CURRENT – A downpouring of Anami's essence that manifests as Light and Sound; unwritten law and the unspoken language that flows out of the Godhead, creating, sustaining, and nurturing all life; pure spiritual consciousness; synonymous with the Shabda, the Word, Tao, Nam, Audible Life Stream, Logos, River of God, Holy Spirit, the Voice of God, Music of the Spheres; power of divine love in expression; expressed as symphonic melodies, and experienced as spontaneous realizations, insights, direct perceptions, solutions, clarified understanding, and heightened viewpoints.

SPIRIT – See: *SOUND CURRENT; SOUL.*

SPIRITUAL CONSCIOUSNESS – Matured consciousness of soul; the goal of the chela's moment-by-moment life.

SPIRITUAL EVOLUTION – Movement into our spiritual nature, in contrast to our primitive human and psychic natures; ultimate attainment in human life; commences via initiation by a living Sat Guru; leads to the emancipation of soul; until this stage, mechanical evolution and karma irrevocably guide one's experience in the lower worlds.

SPIRITUAL EXERCISES – Practices recommended by the Living Master through which all spiritual faculties are discovered, collected, purified, awakened, and emancipated; means that allow one's consciousness to change and one's spiritual objectives to be realized; the deliberate practice of placing one's attention at the third eye center in loving devotion; taught by all true Masters.

SPIRITUAL REALIZATION – Soul's recognition of the real Inner Master; the realization of self as Shabda; the bridge between Self Realization and God Realization.

SPIRITUAL SCIENCE – The essence of the Divine (Shabda) blended with the precise and measurable application of the Teachings, allowing for individual experimentation, direct experience, and the freedom of unbiased assessment.

SPIRITUAL SENSES – Soul's senses of seeing and hearing, in contrast to the five physical senses and to the mental senses that can only conceptualize soul, Spirit, God, and Its emissaries.

SPIRITUALITY – Pursuit of absolute truth; essence of truth that is caught, not taught; life impulses experienced through learning the secrets of truth and applying them in one's daily life.

SRI – Title of veneration and spiritual respect or honor; in Sanskrit, king or sire; denotes an exalted height of spiritual attainment.

SRI GARY OLSEN – Living Sat Guru; founder and spiritual leader of MasterPath, a contemporary expression of the Light and Sound Teachings; incarnated into the Western culture to establish the purity of Sound in the contemporary Western setting; 1948 – present.

STARS, SUN, AND MOON WORLDS – The three inner regions that must be crossed and penetrated before rendezvousing with the Radiant Form of the Master; best understood as currents, or powers, rather than celestial or planetary bodies.

STATE OF CONSCIOUSNESS – Any state or condition that is divided from the unified whole of consciousness; always temporal and unreal in contrast to unified, real, and eternal.

SUBCONSCIOUS MIND – One of the three minds (conscious, subconscious, unconscious); expresses itself in unconscious attitudes, emotional reactivity, habitual behaviors, compulsive attachment to pleasure, aversion to pain, and a host of subtle tendencies.

SURAT SHABDA YOGA – Surat is soul consciousness, Shabda is the essence of the divine Sound Current, and yoga is spiritual practice – hence, the practice of merging soul into the Shabda; the ancient tradition of the Light and Sound Teachings, taught by all true Masters. See: MASTERPATH.

SWATEH SAINT – See: PARAM SAINT.

—T—

THIRD EYE – Tisra til; spiritual heart; eye center; spiritual organ of perception located in the astral body behind and between the eyebrows; wicket gate; upon initiation, the inner form of the Outer Guru stations Himself in this center as the Radiant Form of the Master.

THROAT CHAKRA – Fifth chakra in the physical body; ruled by the power of delusion; seat of philosophical pursuits; worldly intelligence.

TISRA TIL – See: THIRD EYE.

TRANSLATION – Spiritual description of physical death.

TRIKUTI – Second level of Heaven.

TRUE SELF – See: SOUL.

TRUTH – The reality of God, the Master, and the Sound Current; that which is revealed by the Master as consciousness, is transferred to the chela, and is implemented in one's life; the conscious experience of recognizing what the opposites have in common; the middle road; truth does not exist in the lower worlds – only its reflection through the pairs of opposites.

TWO FACES OF THE MASTER – Outer Master and Inner Master; Outer Master models, teaches, and guides through the written and spoken Works; Inner, or Radiant, Master stations Himself in the third eye upon initiation, reveals the unspoken, unwritten, inner Path, and is with His chelas for eternity.

—U—

UNCONSCIOUS MIND – See: *DIVINE MIND*.

UNFOLDMENT – The slow and steady process that removes the sheaths covering the soul (physical, astral, mental, causal, and soul bodies), revealing the vital essence of soul's pure love and bliss; soul's movement from light into Sound, and from mind to soul.

UNIVERSAL MIND – See: *DIVINE MIND*.

UNIVERSAL MIND POWER – Light; duality; the mind in all three of its expressions (conscious, subconscious, and unconscious); reflection of truth that exists as a shadow of reality.

—V—

VANITY – One of the five passions of the mind; at the core of all passions, and the last to be released; self-promotion; insincerity; separation is the primary agenda.

VIEWPOINT – Particular angle of vision chosen when viewing any experience; perspective; determines the quality of one's perceptions; clouded by illusion and maya at the beginning of the spiritual journey; purified to view truth in all things.

VISION – Esoterically, witnessing truth revealed in intuitive imagery; viewed in the third eye center as a pertinent revelation graced by the Sat Guru in response to the disciplined efforts of a chela; exoterically used to promote psychic phenomena facilitating the dominion of the universal mind power and the suppression of Shabda.

VOW – Reciprocal agreement of the initiates of a Living Master; divinely ordained and specifically tailored by the Living Master to enhance the spiritual progression of His initiates.

—W—

WHEEL OF EIGHTY-FOUR – Esoteric representation of soul's journey through the 8,400,000 different life forms in the lower worlds; the cycle of birth and death required for the vast process of soul's maturation as it experiences the myriad karmic conditions indigenous to each different species.

WORD – See: *SOUND CURRENT*.

—Y—

YOGA – Literally, union; esoterically, a spiritual exercise, practice, or system that leads to or aims toward the union of soul with God; exoterically, it is reflected by the universal mind power into many pursuits that stress physical postures and practices, none of which awaken soul.

YUGA – Vast, incomprehensible cycle of time.